Italy

Managing Editor Chris Milsome
Editor Chester Fisher
Assistant Editor Dale Gunthorp
Design Patrick Frean
Picture Research Ed Harriman
Illustration John Shackell
      John Mousdale
      Tony Payne
      Marilyn Day
      Eric Jewel
Maps Matthews & Taylor Associates
Diagrams Ron Hayward
Research aid Giovanna Stefancich

Photographic sources Key to positions
of illustrations: (T) top, (C) centre,
(B) bottom, (L) left, (R) right
A.F.A. Colour Library: *41(TR)* Alitalia:
32(C) Associated Press: *37(C)* Bodleian
Library: *12(BL), 30(T)* Camera Press:
23(C) J. Allan Cash: *32(C)* Central Press
Photographs: *19(TL)* Courtauld
Institute: *12(B), 28(B), 29(TL), 42(B)*
Colorsport: *18(T), 19(B)* Colour Library
International: *2-3, 43(TR)* Daily
Telegraph: *38(C)* Mary Evans Picture
Library: *9(BR), 22(T), 42(C), 43(BR),
44(BL), 45(B)* David Gould: *9(BL)*

Henry Grant: *11(B), 28(B)* Sonia Halliday
Photographs: *8(B), 8(T), 9(TL), 36(B),
40(B), 41(TL)* Ed Harriman: *14(TL),
50(BR), 52(BL)* Imperial War Museum,
London: *47(CR)* Keystone Press Agency:
*17(BR), 19(TL), 19(CL), 19(CR),
35(TL)* Lamborghini: *36(T)* Geoffrey
Magnay: *18(B)* Frederico Arborio Mella:
44(TL) National Gallery, London: *28(T),
29(BR)* Pictor: *22(B), 51(TL), 53(TR)*
Picturepoint: *11(TR), 23(B), 49(TR)*
Popperfoto: *46(BL)* Radio Times Hulton
Picture Library: *26(CL), 27(BL), 30(B),
31(B), 45(TL), 45(TR), 47(TL)* Rex
Features: *17(CL), 17(CR), 52(BR)* Scala:
*8(CL), 25(TL), 42(T), 43(B), 44(B),
48(T)* Nick Scott: *16(T), 16(B), 17(CL),
21(TL), 21(TR), 21(BR), 22(BL),
32(B), 33(CR), 33(B), 38(BR), 39(TL),
39(B), 40(BL), 51(TR)* Servizio Editoriale
Fotografico: *4-5, 11(TR), 14(BR),
15(T), 15(CL), 15(B), 20(T), 21(TL),
24(B), 25(BR), 33(CL), 34(C), 38(CL),
39(TR), 46(CL), 46(C), 53(BR)*
Spectrum: *12(T)* Tate Gallery, London:
29(TR) Thomson Holidays: *45(BR)*
Roger Viollet: *13(TL), 31(T), 31(C),
47(B)* Reg Wilson Photography: *26(B)*

First published 1974
Macdonald Educational Limited
Holywell House
London, E. C. 2

© Macdonald Educational
Limited 1974

Published in the United States
by Silver Burdett Company,
Morristown, N.J.
1981 Printing

ISBN 0 382 06107 1
Library of Congress
Catalog Card No. 75-44863

Italy

the land and its people

Michael Leech

Silver Burdett Company

Contents

The cradle of Europe

Etruscans and Romans

To most people ancient Italy means Rome. The Roman Empire once spread like a stain of the Imperial purple from Africa to Britain and the Romans took their civilization and culture wherever they went, benefiting a multitude of peoples. But even before them came a remarkable race called the Etruscans, who may have been the very first Italians.

Tuscany was their base, and they ruled Rome itself, supposedly founded in 753 B.C. Taken over by the new Romans, the Etruscans vanished and now are only known by their beautiful sculpture and works of art, much influenced by the Greeks.

Foreign influences

The Greeks had established colonies in Southern Italy as far as Naples, which was itself a Greek city. Greek still lingers in the names of cities such as Sybaris (now Sibari), whose ancient inhabitants so loved luxury that even today luxury lovers are called "sybarites".

After these peoples came Phoenicians from Asia and Africa, Arabs, and Normans who had originated in Scandinavia and settled in France. Over the high Alpine passes in the north poured Gauls from the west and nomads from the Danube valley.

All these people brought new ideas and influences—and at first they stayed in their own groups. Before long however, the long mixing began which has resulted in the Italians we know today.

▲ Found in an Etruscan temple, this head is a fine example of the art of this mysterious people whose language is not understood.

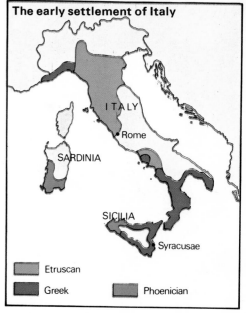

The early settlement of Italy

ITALY

Rome

SARDINIA

SICILIA

Syracusae

☐ Etruscan
☐ Greek   ☐ Phoenician

◄ A Graeco-Roman theatre in Taormina in Sicily. Some of the most splendid Greek buildings are found in southern Italy.

◀ A detail from a hunting scene in mosaic, dating from the third century A.D. The Romans adorned their buildings with works of art. Rich villas often had mosaic floors.

▶ This is a statue of Nero. His pose with sword and armour is designed to impress. The Romans first copied Greek masterpieces, then gradually evolved a style of their own.

▼ Petrified bodies, excavated from the ruins of Herculaneum and Pompei are a reminder of the day Mt. Vesuvius erupted in 76 A.D. burying these rich cities and their citizens in lava and hot ash. The Roman way of life was vividly preserved.

▲ A service in the Catacombs of Rome in 50 A.D. Early Christians were often forced to hide to escape persecution.

Simplicity and splendour

Physical features

Italy is a long, lean peninsula, a leg in a high-heeled boot, Sicily at its toe and Sardinia at its knee. Four-fifths of the country is mountainous—the Alps girdle the north and down the centre runs the long spine of the Apennines. Live volcanoes such as Vesuvius and Etna menace the local inhabitants.

There are more than 2,000 miles of winding coastline. Around Genoa it forms the Riviera, and at the Bay of Naples it provides some of the most superb scenery in the world. The climate ranges from cold in the heights to drought in the south as well as occasional cruel local winds.

In the valley of the Po, Italy's largest river, are rich farms growing rice and cereals; yet the southern provinces, once the prize of the Mediterranean, are now denuded and barren in many places.

Old and new

In the north, industrial prosperity has created a new squalor—chaotic development, ugly buildings and pollution.

Modern roads, some of the best-engineered in Europe, run alongside farms where bullocks are still used to haul carts. Italy has an excellent rail system and busy ports, yet the narrow streets of her old towns were designed for horses. Now they reverberate to the angry buzz of motor-scooters.

Although it is one of the oldest of civilized nations, Italy has only been a unified country since 1860. Before that the city-states fought bitterly amongst each other or indulged in extravagant acts of pride. The towers of the medieval cities are an example—to this day the Siennese are proud that their City Hall tower is higher than that of the Palazzo della Signoria in Florence!

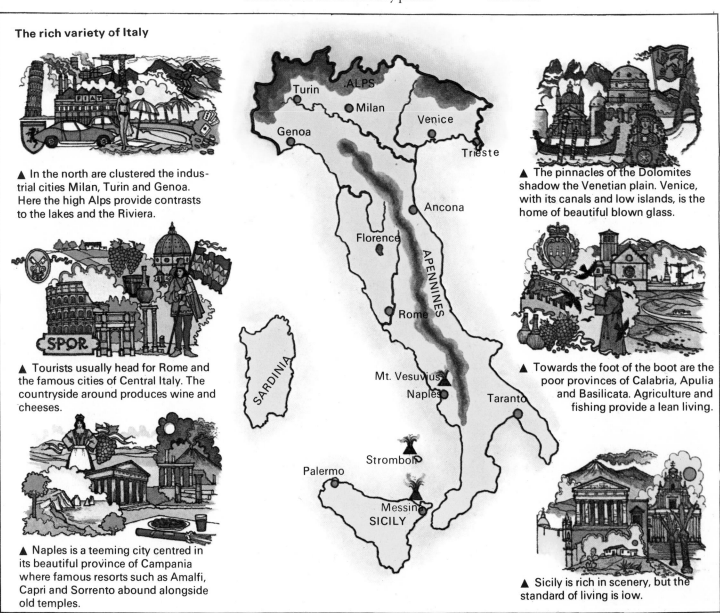

The rich variety of Italy

▲ In the north are clustered the industrial cities Milan, Turin and Genoa. Here the high Alps provide contrasts to the lakes and the Riviera.

▲ Tourists usually head for Rome and the famous cities of Central Italy. The countryside around produces wine and cheeses.

▲ Naples is a teeming city centred in its beautiful province of Campania where famous resorts such as Amalfi, Capri and Sorrento abound alongside old temples.

▲ The pinnacles of the Dolomites shadow the Venetian plain. Venice, with its canals and low islands, is the home of beautiful blown glass.

▲ Towards the foot of the boot are the poor provinces of Calabria, Apulia and Basilicata. Agriculture and fishing provide a lean living.

▲ Sicily is rich in scenery, but the standard of living is low.

▲ Italy is a country of many high mountains. In the Alpine north it is very similar to its neighbours, Switzerland and Austria. Trentino was once part of Austria and German is still spoken in the high valleys.

◄ The centres of Italian cities are often crowded with narrow twisting streets, like this one in Naples. Never designed for modern vehicles, in some cities streets have been closed to motor traffic.

▼ Always close by, the coastline offers a wide variety of scenery. Italians love their beautiful beaches and in summer they are always crowded. Fishing is still an important industry and small boats put out from the little ports to bring rich harvests back to the table.

How the north and south view each other

▲ A misconceived, but popular, view of the southern Italian by northerners is that they are dirty, dishonest and lazy peasants only too happy to depend on support from the north.

▲ Equally at fault is the southern impression of the northerners. It is often held that the northerner is hard and grasping, a greedy businessman lacking in philosophy.

The Italian influence

Roman achievements, Etruscan skills

The ancient peoples of Italy made many contributions to the rest of the world. The Romans were great engineers and they brought their disciplined legions to battle along straight Roman roads, many of which are still used today. They set up well-planned towns with houses that had central heating under their mosaic floors.

Their architecture is still marvelled at and their language, Latin, is the root of many of the modern European tongues. The calendar as we know it is not very different from the one reformed by Julius Caesar to include twelve months, one of them being named after him.

The Etruscans were highly skilled craftsmen. They were fine workers in gold and other metals, and even found how to make sets of false teeth! Their kings were the first to wear crowns and golden rings. They treated women as men's equals and they may have introduced the horse-drawn carriage into Italy.

The Church in Italy

Italy has, of course, been the hub of Roman Catholicism since the early days when the Pope had his seat in Rome and extended a tremendous influence over millions of believers around the world.

The Church was also the first to give patronage to artists, who were set to work adorning churches and later the palaces of prelates and princes. In turn the artist's activities promoted the great revolution in art that we call the Renaissance.

Italians abroad

Italians have emigrated to all corners of the world, many from the poverty-stricken south. They have settled in the United States, Australia, South Africa, and Canada, and to a smaller extent throughout Europe.

▲ Hadrian's Wall in northern England kept the savage Picts and Scots out of Roman Britain.
▼ With manuscripts like these, the Benedictines, an Italian order of monks, kept learning alive through the Dark Ages.

Some Italian gifts to the world

◄ Opera was born in Italy. The greatest singers came from there and now artists go to Italy to learn, hoping that one day they will sing at such theatres as La Scala in Milan or the San Carlo Theatre in Naples. Italian audiences are very demonstrative and the traditional operas are most popular.

▲ People of Italian origin are found in many countries. Here emigrants prepare to leave for America to seek a new life.

▼ A superb picture of the Renaissance, *The Birth of Venus* by Sandro Botticelli, is in the Uffizi Museum, Florence.

► Italian films have gained rapid acceptance since World War II and film-making is now a big industry, based in Rome. Outside Italy usually only the best and most artistic films featuring major stars are known, but many grade B movies and films for Italian television are also made.

◄ Fashion is a fairly new industry for Italy, even though Italians have always had a special flair for clothes. Using dramatic designs the new designers have attracted attention to Rome as a centre of fashion challenging Paris. Leather and wool are often featured.

► The range of architecture in Italy is so immense that a book could hardly contain it. Styles range from Roman and Greek to Byzantine and Romanesque; from Gothic and Renaissance to Baroque and Palladian and there is a great interest in modern building often using materials in unusual ways.

◄ Furniture and household articles receive special attention from Italian designers. For example they use plastics with great imagination, and many pieces are made to stack and fit into each other. Glassware, machinery, cars and jewellery also get the special design touch.

The changing role of the family

▲ Italians love their children and spend hours playing with them indoors and out.

Powerful families

In Italy, perhaps more than in any other European country, the family comes first. Families have shaped the history of the country—the Renaissance rulers such as the Sforzas of Milan, the Gonzagas of Mantua or the d'Este family of Ferrara. Each governed a city state, taking their cue from the Pope himself. For Pope Alexander VI used his position to help his children, Cesare and Lucrezia Borgia. Nepotism, or helping your relations, was not at all unusual in high places.

Even today, in Sicily and parts of the south, feuds between different families smoulder and break into fights. "The Family" is the name given to the Mafia, the organization of power-hungry men which started in Italy and whose interests, often associated with crime, circle the globe. Within the Mafia, different families control different areas.

The family at home

Although modern life is breaking up the family unit and more and more young couples start married life in a place of their own, it is still a great Italian pleasure to congregate with relations for a large meal.

In the country families still live together, the sons bringing their wives to live in the main house and the grandmother, or older aunts looking after the children while the parents work. Italians love large families (unfortunately birth control is not much practised) and in poor districts the sons will sometimes leave for foreign countries in order to find work. Each week they send money home, and so the family closeness is maintained.

A typical family timetable

8.00 a.m.

8.30 a.m.

9.00 a.m.

1.00 p.m.

2.00 p.m.

4.00 p.m.

5.00 p.m.

7.30 p.m.

8.30 p.m.

9.00 p.m.

11.00 p.m.

▲ In Friuli, east of Venice, workers lunch in a cafeteria. Although many no longer go home for a midday meal, they still eat heartily and drink the customary wine.

▲ A traditionally furnished flat or house. The daughter plays by the gilt table while the son does his homework. Shutters keep out noise at nights and strong sun by day.

▶ Whenever possible the family eats together —here father, mother and children are taking *pranzo*, or lunch, for which a long break is allowed. Children take wine with water and there is always lots of fruit and cheese.

◀ In common with most other countries of Europe, television is popular although there is only a black-and-white service at present. Even the dog is part of the audience!

An average family budget

Food, drink and tobacco   35.4%

Housing, light and fuel   15.1%

Transport and   10.4% communications

Clothing and footwear   8.8%

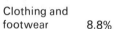

Taxes and   8.5% national insurance

Goods and services   7.1%

Education and entertainment   6.6%

Household furnishing and upkeep   5.7%

Health, hygiene 2.4%

Leisure and pleasure

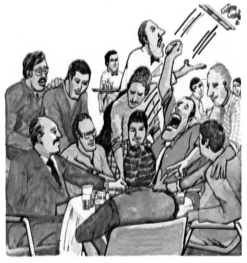

Sociable People

One of the most attractive things about the Italians is the way they maintain a warm interest in each other, and especially within their families. If Granny, or *la nonna* as she is called, does not live with the family then at weekends visits are made with gifts of flowers and sweets.

Children are very important in Italy and a lot of time is spent with them—they are often to be seen sitting at dinner tables quite late in the evening, their fond parents treating them like small adults.

Italians are all very sociable—and both men and women love to congregate in cafes for a chat and a look at the passers-by. In smaller towns there is a well-established custom called the *passeggio*. This is a parade, mostly of the younger men and girls, which takes place on a certain central street or *piazza* in the evenings. The girls put on their best clothes and the men, also in their best, compliment them with glances and comments.

The barber-shops in smaller towns are almost as important as cafes to Italian life. Frequently they are gathering places to chat, read the latest magazines and papers, and relax while the customers, both men and women, are fussed over.

Sports and pastimes

Television and radio are important, but many prefer a game of cards. Outdoor enthusiasts like to fish and shoot. Tennis is popular and so are winter sports which are coming within the range of the less well-off. However, fencing, sculling and riding are still the preserve of the rich. Many large towns have covered arcades, like the *Galleria* in Milan, and here there is a kind of *passeggio* all day long.

▲ The cafe in Italy is a kind of a club. Eating and drinking are almost secondary, and patrons linger for hours with talk, reading and playing various games.

▶ Glossy periodicals are popular in Italy. However, newspapers are not read widely, although Milan and Rome possess prestigious ones. It is estimated that 40 per cent of all families do not read a book or paper.

▼ Walking, talking and meeting friends in the street are pursuits dear to all Italians and the cities are lively with laughter and conversations. Dogs must wait while their owners read or just chat. Street entertainments include bands and strolling performers.

Some popular pastimes

▲ A visit to Granny by the family is a special occasion. Family life is of great importance.

▲ Shooting is very popular. Even the smallest birds and animals are targets.

▲ Like the café, the hairdresser's is a place to socialize and catch up on news and gossip.

A typical day on television

Italian television, *Radio-Audizioni Italiane* (RAI/TV), has two channels which are both state sponsored with some commercial advertising. Programmes are varied and cover films, plays, children's programmes, sports and newscasts. Although the studios have colour equipment, there is as yet no colour transmission in Italy.

9 a.m.-12 noon. **Schools programmes**
1 p.m. **News bulletin**
2 p.m.-5 p.m. **Schools programmes**
Until this point only one channel is in operation.
5 p.m.-6.30 p.m. **Programmes for children.** Periods of 30 minutes are devoted to different age groups.

During the evening the first channel broadcasts short news bulletins at the end of programmes.

7 p.m.-8.30 p.m. **Cultural programmes**
8.30 p.m. **The news** the major news broadcast of the day
8.50-9 p.m. **Carosello** the most popular programme on Italian T.V. It acts as an alarm clock for children as they are sent to bed at the end.
9 p.m. **Evening programmes** which may be films, plays, music or light entertainment.
11 p.m. (approximately) **News** and closedown.

Famous Italian entertainers

▲ A fine actress as well as a striking beauty Sophia Loren is almost an Italian trademark. She has her country's flair for clothes and is also an unconventional woman.

▲ Marcello Mastroianni is certainly one of the best known film stars in and out of his country. His handsome, brooding looks are in a special Italian vein.

▲ In Italy, like everywhere else, the music of the 1960s produced a new kind of performer. One such pop idol is Gulliver, who could belong to any Western country.

▲ A Roman, Alberto Sordi comes from a working-class background. He plays many different characters and brings his special, city humour to them all.

Sport
a great passion

National sports

One of the greatest passions of the Italian people is sport. Whether racing along narrow city streets on motor scooters or watching a big football match on television, the average Italian spends a great number of his leisure hours on sport. It is considered so important that there is a special government department to coordinate sports activities—the National Olympic Committee.

This organization also supervises the construction of sports grounds and gymnasiums. These range from such buildings as the Sports Palace at Bologna to the Light Athletics Stadium at Palermo, from covered swimming pools in Trieste to the Winter Olympic Games complex at Cortina d'Ampezzo.

Winter sports—skiing, skating and bob-sledding—are popular in the many mountain areas, but the most popular sport is football or *calcio*. All the large cities have teams, and a major game can draw huge crowds. Bicycle racing is also high on the list. Although there have been spectacular accidents which resulted in some government curbs, motor car racing is another major interest.

Gambling and hunting

Betting on sports events is an Italian passion and there are national pools for soccer, greyhound and horse racing and also a national lottery. Italians spend billions of lire each week, some of which help pay for the Olympic Committee's activities. Richer Italians visit racetracks, watch show-jumping, play tennis, and fence. For those with no money card-games are popular, as is the game of *bocce* or bowls.

Italians are eager hunters. Sadly they decimate the flocks of small birds on migration from North Africa to Europe.

▲ The badge of the Juventus Football Club. Juventus is one of the strongest and most popular Italian teams. It was founded in 1897 and is known in Italy as 'The Grand Old Lady'. The Club is based in Turin and gets much financial support from the owners of the giant Fiat motor company. Juventus were Italian League champions in 1960, 1961, 1967 and 1972. They won the Italian Cup in 1960 and 1965.

▶ Every Sunday the huge football stadiums of Milan, Naples, Turin and Rome fill with thousands of eager fans. Shown here is an international match between Italy and Brazil.

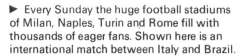

▲ The Italians design superb sports cars capable of very high speeds. Auto racing is one of the most popular of sports and appeals to Italian temperament, combining sleek machines, daredevil drivers and thrills—sometimes leading to tragic accidents.

Great Italian sportsmen

▲ Riva, the great footballer, plays for Cagliari and the Italian team.

▲ Grimondi, world cycling champion, won the Tour de France in 1965.

▲ G. Agostini, world motorcycle champion, has won 13 major titles.

▲ Panatta, Italy's tennis champion, is one of the world's top players.

▼ The Monza auto circuit is one the most famous in the world. Situated to the north-east of Milan, on the way to the Lakes, it is the scene of the Italian Grand Prix.

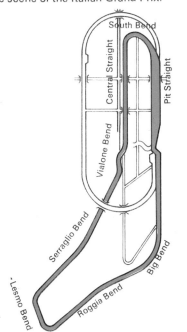

South Bend

Central Straight

Pit Straight

Vialone Bend

Serraglio Bend

Big Bend

Lesmo Bend

Roggia Bend

▶ A famous horseman, Piero d'Inzeo, takes a fence. Show-jumping attracts much interest though it is mainly an upper-class sport.

Educating a nation

Kindergarten to *Liceo*

Most children in Italy go to public schools where they are entitled to at least eight years of free education. Some children go to kindergarten before they reach the age for entry to the elementary school. After five years at this grade they enter the *Scuola Media*, or middle school.

By law a secondary school must exist in every town with a population of more than 3,000. However, after their secondary school period, many pupils go on to a *Liceo*, or grammar school, for up to five years. Others go to technical schools to learn a trade—there are commercial schools, agricultural schools and many varieties of industrial training.

There are special technical institutes for women and girls, offering courses in welfare and social science. Many students take four-year courses to become elementary school teachers. Those who went to the *Liceo* take examinations and often enter universities.

Universities

There are 36 cities with universities throughout the country. Italy possesses one of the oldest universities in the world—Bologna, founded in 1135. Other old and famous ones are to be found at Pisa, Pavia and Padua. The largest is in Rome. At the universities there are many foreign students, attracted by Italian government grants as well as by the high standards. Training in the arts is given at special institutes providing a three-year course. These began in the workshops and corporations of the middle ages.

The arts play an important part in everyday life and drama, music and dancing are taught at many professional academies. Rome possesses a film training school that has been in existence since the 1930s.

▲ Children leaving school at the end of a day at Volpiano in Piedmont. More than 4 million children attend elementary schools. To house the greatly increased numbers, a large building programme has taken place in the last twenty years.

The Italian school system

Female enrolments in universities only began in large numbers in 1945.

University 18+

▲ Italy has made a determined effort in recent years to improve standards of education. Even so standards of literacy are low when compared with many other countries. Southern Italy has special problems as facilities are often inadequate. In addition, most universities, museums, and academies of art and music are found in the north.

▲ Schoolgirls in uniform going to school near the Pantheon seem from a different world as they troop past the patrons of a café.

▲ At fifteen students can choose a professional training school if he or she wishes. Here a student in Rome learns to type.

▲ Italians are conscientious parents and often interest themselves actively in what is being taught at school. Here a young boy asks his father questions about homework.

▶ A state school in Rome. Education is controlled by the Ministry in Rome and is a a relic of an attempt to create a national culture at the time of unification.

The Church
a social force

Roman Catholicism

One of the most important buildings in any Italian town is the church. Whether it be the splendid spikey Gothic cathedral of Milan or a tiny mountain church in the Dolomites, it has a special significance for the people who live around it. Religion is a great influence on the life of many Italians, who often unquestioningly accept troubles as a sign of divine displeasure. The majority (97 per cent) of Italians are Roman Catholics and many of those see their church as a haven in times of trouble.

Roman Catholicism is declared in the Constitution as the state religion, although other creeds are permitted. Catholic religious teaching is given in the elementary schools, but the government has the right to approve the appointments of bishops and archbishops.

The Pope is the head of the Roman Catholic Church and resides in the Vatican, a tiny state within the boundaries of Rome. He has tremendous power as the originator of doctrines and opinions. His followers number more than 300 millions around the world, and at certain periods, such as a Holy Year, as many as five million pilgrims come to the Vatican to pray at St. Peter's.

Parish festivals

No less important to the people is their parish priest, a man to whom they turn at all times. The churches themselves are often sumptuously decorated, contrasting with the poor housing of the parish. Processions and pilgrimages, special events such as christenings, weddings or first communions, are celebrated with much pomp and feasting.

Fireworks and illuminations often form part of religious festivals—in Florence, on Easter Eve, the Archbishop frees an artificial dove which flies on wires to the cathedral door, where a huge bonfire is prepared on a cart. The dove ignites the fire and fireworks explode to the delight of huge crowds.

▲ During the early days of Christianity many fell in the Colosseum. Wild animals sometimes tore Christian martyrs to pieces.

▼ A girl in Messina goes to church for her first communion. Such events are important milestones in Italian life.

▲ This figure of a saint is carried through the streets of a southern town with his head and shoulders draped in live snakes to ward off evil.

▼ High mass inside the biggest church in the world—St. Peter's. The twisted columns of the *baldacchino* surround the high altar.

The Vatican—home of the Pope

The Vatican State is the smallest in the world to which other countries send ambassadors. The permanent population is little more than a thousand and the Pope is its head. The Vatican is a collection of buildings, partly surrounded by a wall. Within the city are St. Peter's, the Sistine Chapel, palaces, offices, libraries, art galleries and barracks for the Swiss Guard.

▼ Pope John Paul II, seen here on his 1979 visit to Mexico.

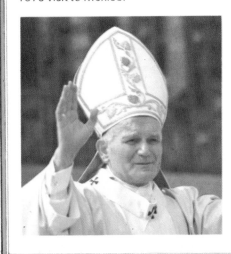

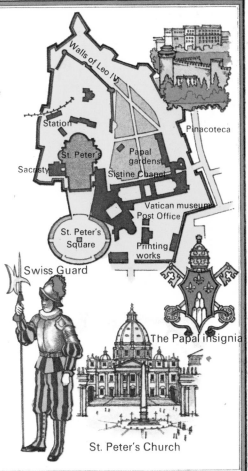

Walls of Leo IV
Station
Pinacoteca
St. Peter's
Sacristy
Papal gardens
Sistine Chapel
Vatican museum
Post Office
St. Peter's Square
Printing works
Swiss Guard
The Papal insignia
St. Peter's Church

▲ The cathedral in Milan is a rarity in Italy—a Gothic building. Its many pinnacles and spires, topped with statues of saints, make an imposing skyline. Because its foundations were being damaged by vibrations, motor traffic is not allowed nearby.

Customs and superstitions

▲ Men will often promenade arm-in-arm while they chat or admire the girls.

▲ Italians "talk" with their hands. This sign means "your head is full of pine cones" (you are a fool).

▲ On greeting kisses are often exchanged and touch contact is important.

The living and the dead

As befits an antique land, Italy is a country of strong prejudices. Many superstitions have clustered in the south—for example women who have fits of hysteria in remote villages are thought to have been bitten by *tarontole*, or devils, represented by poisonous spiders. Treatment is given by the priest. Where people live close to the soil there is a strong belief in the evil eye and witchcraft. Many religious parades have their origins in pagan customs and death is not a distant thing to peasants. On Sundays after Mass you will even see people talking by the graveside as though the dead person were still there.

The dramatic spirit

The theatricality of Italians comes to the fore in a variety of customs and festivals. In Venice on St. Mark's Eve (April 25), women and girls receive from their admirers a rosebud or *boccolo*. In southern wedding processions one still sometimes sees the dowry being carried to make neighbours aware of the riches of the bride. Any occasion is a good one for dressing up—city guilds and clubs re-enact battles in costume —and at Christmas Rome is invaded by shepherds with bagpipes.

▲ A New Year's Eve custom is the getting rid of unwanted things. A rain of rubbish some as big as baths keep revellers wary.

▼ In the province of Vicenza the town of Marostica hosts a game of chess, played every year before the medieval castle. The chessmen are citizens, fantastically costumed.

▼ Instead of Santa Claus, Italy has *La Beffanna*, a little old lady, ugly but wise, who stuffs shoes with gifts on Epiphany. Held on January 6, Epiphany celebrates the visit to Christ of the Three Kings.

Italian superstitions

▲ Gnocchi are small round potato dumplings. Eating them on September 29 brings luck.

▲ Chrysanthemums in Italy are *only* for graves, and they are always associated with funerals.

▲ Local citizens costume themselves for the *Palio*, a traditional horse race held in the middle of Sienna. Thousands watch the event, which only takes two minutes!

▼ Southern Italy is a country of many conventions. People wear black, and although women may be central at home, men dominate public and social life, as in this Sicilian setting.

The excitement of opera

▲ Giuseppe Verdi was the son of an innkeeper but rose to be one of the best known opera composers. *Il Trovatore, Aida, Rigoletto* and *La Traviata* are performed world-wide.

▼ A scene from Verdi's opera *Aida*, at La Scala in Milan. La Scala is possibly the most famous opera house in the world.

Italy—the home of opera

Although all the arts have blossomed at different times in Italy, opera is the most distinctively Italian. It is very difficult to describe exactly what opera *is*—perhaps that is why when the great composer Monteverdi wrote the first one in the seventeenth century it was called *opera* which in Italian means "work". Opera is usually based on a play or a book; the lines of the drama, called the *libretto*, are almost always sung. After a rousing or romantic overture there is usually lots of swirling, dramatic action, set against elaborate scenery. Opera requires a full orchestra, a large chorus and leading singers, whole ballet companies to dance during the action and an army of backstage technicians to ensure smooth working. It is therefore a very expensive art. In the past it was a favourite entertainment at the courts of kings. Indeed it needed a rich man to pay the bills! Even today it is a costly hobby for those buying tickets at the famous opera houses.

A popular art

Today opera is a pleasure shared by millions of Italians. As an indication of how widespread it is, you will hear popular arias and overtures on radio or television, and even sung by people on the street.

Italy has many great opera houses and in summer you can also hear it in the arenas of Verona and Rome. Many of the great composers were Italian and the leading singers of today were often born there. Some, like the great tenor Caruso, started in poverty and became rich through their golden voices.

Music and colour

It is true that when attending an opera, one has to "suspend disbelief"; the hero is often decidedly plump, while the soprano may seem far too healthy to die of wasting disease at the end of Act IV. But Italians nevertheless sit back to enjoy the colour and action, the glorious singing and music, applauding loudly with cries of *bravi* if they feel like it, or shouting *boo* if they think the singer is not good enough for their opera house.

▲ It is part of an Italian's character to express himself when he feels like it. In Venice *gondolieri* sing arias while they work.

▲ Opera singers have the popularity of film stars. Fans wait at backstage doors and at performances 'claques' applaud favourites.

▲ A poster announcing a production at one of the world's great opera houses—La Scala in Milan. Opera is usually presented in repertory—that is different productions on consecutive nights.

▼ The great tenor Caruso was born in poverty but his golden voice, which we can still hear on record, made his fortune.

▲ Opera is an old-fashioned art, using nineteenth century scenic effects. Here the backstage workings can be seen—the lights, lines for moving sets and a costume ready for a quick change. The conductor is the dictator from whom all take their cue.

A great artistic tradition

Inheritors of the Renaissance

From the monuments of ancient Rome, Greece and Etruria to the modern sculptures of Marino Marini, Italians have always been surrounded by art. Examples of Italian art can be found not only in churches and museums, but also in the streets of old towns, like Verona. Skilled artists in wood, metal and fabrics can be seen in their tiny workshops, carrying on a tradition that began in the middle ages.

The Renaissance, or *Rinascimento*, which means rebirth, started in Florence. It was a great upsurge in the artistic life of Europe. It affected painting, sculpture, architecture, poetry, music, literature and also science. It produced such great Italians as Leonardo da Vinci, Michelangelo, Giotto, Dante, Donatello, Palestrina and Vivaldi.

A creative land

Everybody was affected by the Renaissance. Even tyrants employed artists to paint pictures, scholars to translate Latin manuscripts, and architects to design buildings. The results can still be seen today, for example, in the many Italian-style buildings of London and Boston. If Leonardo's plans for flood control had been put into effect, Florence might never have had the disastrous floods of 1966.

Patrons of art during the Renaissance were often lavish and sometimes wasteful. Painters would design masques, ballets and processions while the Republic of Venice employed renowned sculptors to create works in edible materials for banquets!

The church has always been a great patron of the arts and many are treasure houses of ninth century mosaics, Romanesque sculptures, medieval frescoes, baroque decorations and eighteenth century paintings.

Opera is an Italian art, and so is some ballet. Theatre has always been most important, with a tradition stretching back many centuries. Immortal figures like Harlequin and Columbine, Pantalone and Punchinello (our modern Mr. Punch) come from Italy.

▲ Recently Titian's canvas of *Bacchus and Ariadne,* depicting one of the legends of the gods, was cleaned. It shows the glorious hues used by the artist who died in 1576, the greatest painter of the Venetian High Renaissance.

▶ Bernini's statues and fountains are to be seen all over Rome. This is part of the Four Rivers fountain in the Piazza Navona.

▼ Michelangelo's painting of the Prophet Isaiah from the Sistine Chapel. The ceiling, the story of Genesis, took four years to paint.

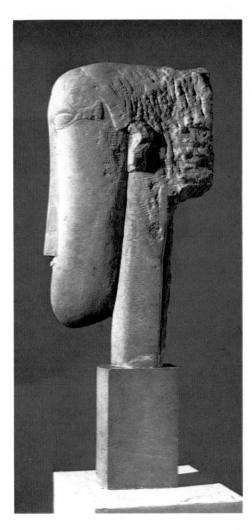

▲ Dante Alighieri, the father of the Italian language, met Beatrice when they were both nine years old. This Victorian picture makes them much older. She was his lifelong inspiration.

▶ Amadeo Modigliani was a painter and sculptor. His works are elongated and sinuous, like this striking head made in 1913.

▼ Venice is still very much today as the eighteenth century painter, known as Canaletto, painted it for rich foreign patrons.

Exploring the unknown

A great tradition

Adventure and excitement have always marked Italy in a special way. Think of the important explorers who came from that country—Marco Polo wending his perilous way over the Silk Route to far-off China; Amerigo Vespucci charting unknown oceans to give his name to the great new continent of America, Christopher Columbus who first set foot on that wild shore.

Nor is exploring limited to these gallant voyagers over the earth—Galileo Galilei spent many hours scanning the heavens to discover new facts and suffered imprisonment for his belief that the earth moved round the sun. Later Guglielmo Marconi experimented with radio, creating widespread excitement when the signals from his lone aerial were first picked up.

Electric and atomic energy

Electricity was discovered by Luigi Galvana of Bologna two centuries ago and the problem of storing this new source of power was solved by Allesandro Volta with his battery. Volta also designed a condenser for producing electricity. Yet another Italian, Antonio Pacinotti, discovered a way of turning a dynamo with electric magnetism and the new power became of immense value to humanity.

It is hard to imagine the world without electricity, but only recently were the new sources of atomic power discovered. In time atomic power may be as important in daily life as coal or oil generated electric power is today. Uranium fission was achieved in 1930 and twelve years later came the first atomic chain reaction. Another Italian, Enrico Fermi had ushered in the Atomic Age.

Marco Polo and the road to China

▼ Nicolo Polo was a thirteenth century Venetian merchant who made the incredibly difficult journey over almost uncharted lands to China and the court of Kublai Khan at Peking. He and his brother were the first Europeans ever seen there. They had been away for nine years when they got back to Venice; yet two years later they made the trip again, this time with Marco, Nicolo's son. Marco became a great favourite of the Khan and travelled all over Asia in his service. His stories, were for many years the only written descriptions of the countries of the Far East.

Leonardo da Vinci—a man ahead of his age

Leonardo da Vinci was an extraordinary man of multiple talents, and of restless and enquiring spirit. Born in Tuscany, he was apprenticed to a painter in Florence in 1469 and went on to become court painter and inventor to the Duke of Milan. Some of his many inventions, for which we have detailed drawings, include armoured cars (its conical cover deflects missiles); diving equipment (the fin is almost exactly the same as those we use today) and wings utilising air-currents, like a glider.

▲ This is taken from a self-portrait of Leonardo, done when he was an old man. In 1516, after painting masterpieces like the Mona Lisa, he went to live in France under the patronage of the French king.

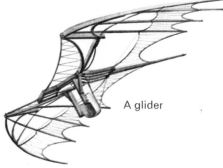

A glider

Galileo and the fight for truth

▲ The story of Galileo Galilei's trial is well known. He had heretically suggested, through his announcement that the planets moved about the sun, that the earth was not the centre of the universe. Under threat of torture he recanted but the legend goes that he stated after the trial 'But it does move'. In 1581 when he was only 17, he observed the movement of pendulums and established that whatever the oscillations they were executed in equal times. His most famous invention was the telescope which he perfected to a power of 32. With it he made many discoveries including the Mountains of the Moon, sunspots, Jupiter's satellites and the phases of Venus. He continually watched the skies until he went blind, yet still worked up to his death in 1642.

▼ Luigi Galvani was a scientist of the eighteenth century. At Bologna, where he was a lecturer in anatomy, he began his famous studies of electrology and magnetism in animals. The experiment illustrated here was conducted with the body of a frog that had been skinned. Galvani was able to observe the passage of an electric current through the animal, by the twitching of muscles occurring at the same time as contact with iron and copper. Constructing a device of two different metals he placed one next to the frog's nerve, the other next to a muscle: the result was the contraction of the muscle. Without knowing it he had produced an electric current.

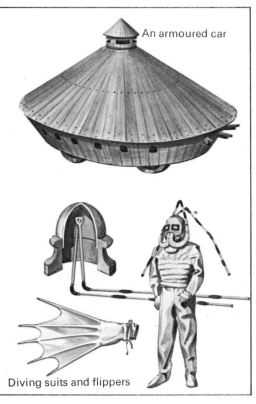

An armoured car

Diving suits and flippers

A great step in communication

▲ Guglielmo Marconi (born 1874) was already transmitting long-wave radio signals when he was 21. He used an induction coil with a spark discharger controlled by a Morse tapping key; a filings coherer formed the receiver. He received little encouragement to continue his work, which after experiments with aerials he was convinced was of major worth. So he went to London where he was offered much more assistance. It was the beginning of broadcasting, radio communications and navigation links. After inventing wireless telegraphy with its short wave system for longer distances, he experimented with sickness cures and in 1909 was awarded the Nobel Prize.

Shopping for the best

Salami and silk

Shopping is done daily for the home. Bakers bake every day and food shops seem to be open all the time, so that you can buy early in the morning or late at night. Only the butcher closes down sometimes for religious festivals and special days. Sweets and cakes are found in great abundance at the *pasticceria* where one also gets aperitifs and after-dinner liqueurs.

A popular spot on any Italian main street is the delicatessen where one can purchase all sorts of hors d'oeuvres, ham, salami and smoked meats. Fruit and vegetable shops, grocers and fishmongers, dairies and poultry shops (where one can buy game in season) are also found. Fashionable shopping streets sell the newest ideas in clothes, and Italian leather goods, shoes and articles of men's wear are world famous. Italian silk is featured in many small boutiques or in large department stores.

Prices are often lower than in other European countries and the choice of goods is wide. The sociable aspect of shopping appeals to the people and the housewife looks forward to her morning ritual, going from shop to shop, comparing prices and purchases and chatting with friends she meets on the way.

▲ Italian markets are a painter's pallet with sun-ripened fruits and vegetables like these peppers, laid in profusion on the stalls. Cooks prefer fresh ingredients for their meals and prepared frozen foods are not as popular as in some other countries.

▲ All sorts of cheeses, often formed into unusual shapes, can be found in markets. Cheese is made from the milk of the goat, sheep, cow and water buffalo. It is a staple food, appearing in many dishes. Provolone, mozzarella, romano are just a few of them.

◀ Although the Italian unit of currency is the lira, it is a very tiny unit and the lowest denomination you will find in your change is a five lire coin. You may feel very rich with a large 10,000 lire banknote but it would only buy a meal for two.

The essential market

▲ Melon is seen everywhere when in season. It is often cut in patterns to attract the buyer.

▲ Hardware stalls still feature old-fashioned brooms, feather dusters, garden implements.

▲ Most food can be found in markets including salamis, sausages and all sorts of ham.

▲ Meat is displayed on marble slabs—and in this shop walls and floor are marble too. Veal and beef are popular meats.

▲ Ice cream, or *gelati*, was invented in Italy in the eighteenth century. To make it then, blocks of ice were stored until summer in deep wells. Now, hygienically-made, one can buy it everywhere in many delicious flavours.

◄ A staple of the diet is fish, in its many forms. Here in the Campo dei Fiori market in Rome trays of shellfish are for sale—mussels are particularly popular and so are *vongole*, or clams. However one must be careful of polluting influences; recent outbreaks of cholera in Naples were traced to infected shellfish.

Eating the Italian way

Great Italian dishes

Don't think for a moment that Italian food is like the tins of spaghetti you see in the supermarket. Italian food, whether sampled in restaurants or in a home, is a most delicious and unique cuisine. Spaghetti is just one variety of 'pasta', and pasta is only one of the great Italian specialities. Real pasta is made fresh every day, like a new-baked loaf. In the north it can be noodles; around Naples it's made into all sorts of shapes from little ears to baby boots! And it is served with dozens of different sauces. The Italian 'mamma' is eternally resourceful.

Italians make marvellous soups, thick and thin, served with crusty bread. Around Bergamo a pudding made of cornmeal called 'polenta' is popular. Near the Yugoslavian border, delicious Italian goulash is made, and in Brindisi roast eel or stuffed kid. The Tuscans like *bue*, or beefsteak. In Piedmont stews are made from chamoix, the mountain antelope. *Fritto di pesce*, a mixed fish fry straight from the Adriatic, is popular in Venice. Fish, veal, chicken and ham are found all over Italy and lots of salads and fresh fruits. Desserts are mouthwatering. From sausages to sweets, Italians love their food and they enjoy seeing the visitor's pleasure in a well-cooked meal.

Typical meals for a day

Breakfast:
7.30 a.m. (weekdays) Coffee only. Occasionally pastries.

Lunch:
Noon (weekdays) — Antipasto. Canneloni
1.30 p.m. (Sundays) — Veal escalope, salad. Chianti. Pears in wine. Espresso.

Coffee:
4 p.m. Coffee, either espresso or capucino

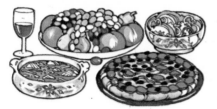

Dinner:
8.30 p.m. Thick fish soup — cacciocco. Pizza. Green salad, with peppers. Fresh fruit.

▲ A modern introduction is the quick service light lunch. Here in Turin, at the *Bar Motta*, businessmen drink the ever-popular *espresso*, strong dark coffee served in small cups.

Some famous regional dishes

Parma Ham with Melon
Ham from Parma is delicious. It is carefully and slowly cured and when ready is shaved off in thin slices, for like so many good things, it is very expensive! It is classically served with melon, or ripe figs. It can be presented as illustrated, with each slice of rich, ripe honeydew melon one or two slices of ham; or cut into cubes with a sliver of ham pinned round it with a toothpick.

Roast lamb with rosemary
Agnello all'aretino is roast lamb as served in the central district of the Latium. Roasted in the oven with rosemary, it is basted with oil and vinegar, red wine or marsala. Cut into thick slices it is served in a sauce made from the juices. Lamb has not always been available on Italian menus; now supplies of New Zealand mutton means cooks can serve it in their distinctive way.

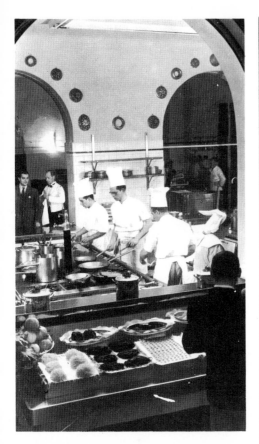

One of Italy's most famous restaurants is Giannino's where the poor of Milan are fed for nothing from the profits of feeding the rich. The modern kitchens are always bustling with activity as dozens of dishes, including specialities from all over Italy, are prepared. They look mouth-watering, for Italians appreciate good food.

Cassata Siciliana

In Italy one must be careful when wishing to order this dessert. When called 'gelato', or ice cream, it is as illustrated, a pudding-shaped mound of different flavoured ice creams with lots of chopped candied fruits and nuts. If a 'dolce', or sweet, it is made of ricotta cheese, studded with fruit, chocolate and cherries, flavoured with vanilla and contained within sponge fingers.

Make yourself an Italian meal

SPAGHETTI AND TOMATO SAUCE
(for 3-4 people)
1 medium tin of tomatoes
1 onion, chopped
2 tbs olive oil
1 garlic clove, chopped
1 carrot, grated
½ pt of stock, beef or chicken
3 level tbs tomato concentrate
Freshly cooked spaghetti
Seasoning—salt, pepper, basil, nutmeg
Grated Parmesan cheese

CHICKEN BREASTS IN CREAM SAUCE
(For 4 people)
4 large chicken breasts
1 medium onion, chopped
3 tbs butter or oil
¾ pt chicken stock
½ lb mushrooms, sliced
Large container of single cream
Salt, pepper, marjoram, chopped parsley
2 tbs plain flour
Juice of ½ lemon
Mixed salad ingredients

COFFEE ICE CREAM WITH NUTS
(For 4 people)
1 container coffee ice cream
2 tablespoons double cream
Almond or nut-flavoured syrup
(if not available use chocolate syrup)
1 cup chopped walnuts

Method
Heat oil in a thick pan. Add onion, garlic and carrot. Fry over low heat for 5 mins. Add the tinned tomatoes. (Or four or five skinned fresh if preferred.) Season with a little salt, ground pepper, pinch nutmeg and basil. Add the concentrate and some stock, topping up as cooking proceeds. Stir with a wooden spoon to prevent sticking. Cook gently for 45 mins. Taste for seasoning. (Sometimes a tsp of brown sugar helps.) Cook spaghetti in a large pan with lots of boiling water to which a little cooking oil has been added. About 2 cups water to each ounce of pasta. Salt well. Cook for 10-12 mins. When done (soft but not soggy) strain and remove to a warmed dish. Heap over the sauce and serve with parmesan.

Method
Heat the butter in a large pan. Add onion and fry gently until golden. Add washed and dried breasts and turn when browned. Add stock and cook gently for 20 minutes, with herbs, salt and freshly-ground pepper. Lift out breasts and place in a casserole in a warm oven. Strain liquid, pressing through a sieve. In the pan, heat oil and quickly fry sliced mushrooms until golden. Sift over flour, adding more oil to cook it if necessary. Stir continually with wooden spoon for 2-3 minutes, then slowly add strained stock and lemon juice. Cook slowly until thick. Add cream, a little at a time, stirring sauce. Taste for flavour. At this point a small glass of white wine can be added. Pour over chicken in casserole and serve at once. Make salad of sliced peppers, fresh lettuce or watercress.
Dressing: oil and vinegar with seasoning such as thyme or mixed herbs, or whisk in a tbs of sour cream.

Method
Place coffee ice cream in a bowl with two tbs of syrup and double cream. With a wooden spoon, mash ice cream and mix with ingredients which need not be completely absorbed. Mix in walnuts, reserving some for topping. Place in tall glasses and serve at once or keep in freezer until needed.

Note: Presentation is always an important point. Nuts and cream on top of the dessert, chopped parsley or sprigs of watercress on the chicken, spaghetti served in a large bowl—all help to make the meal look more attractive.

A genius for style and quality

The Italian flair

A tremendous flair for design is expressed in modern Italian products. Many things are still produced in traditional shapes, such as glass from the lagoon workshops of Venice, or the leather desk sets and straw-work of Florence. But in the fields of furniture, cars and fashions a native ingenuity and love of the dramatic is evident.

New ideas from Italy

New materials are used in exciting ways, such as plastic chairs and stacking storage units. Roman fashion designers make a distinctive Italian look whether they use traditional sumptuous silks or striking new textiles created and woven by artists.

Italian cars are always recognizable for their curving, sporty lines, or for their functional design, as in the case of the popular Fiat. Fiat was created by the remarkable Giovanni Agnelli, who built up and managed what became a great industrial empire until his death. Other important figures in Italian industry are Camillo Olivetti and his son Adriano. Their typewriter company grew, through fine workmanship and sound management, to become the largest business machine manufacturing company in Europe.

Italy produces a great amount of high quality marble. It is a common material used to decorate many apartment buildings.

Products for the table

Foodstuffs include many varieties of prepared meats such as salamis, ham from Parma, brawns and tongue. Italy produces rice and cereals as well as large crops of vegetables and fruits for home consumption and export. Olive oil is crushed from the fruit of the grey olive tree and wine is produced all over the peninsula, as are Italian cheeses.

▲ A Lamborghini sports car, parked in London, illustrates the popularity of this car abroad. Italy exports many fine luxury cars, often of eyecatching design.

▲ Prepared meats are one of Italy's most famous products. Sausages and salamis come in many varieties. Ham makes an appetizer called *prosciutto* when cut into fine slices.

► From the great quarries of Carrara comes the famous marble. Most is used in buildings and Michelangelo selected his stone here.

How Murano glass is made

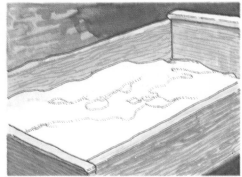

▲ Table glass begins this way, a powdered mixture of silicates and chemicals.

▲ Heated in the furnace it is withdrawn on a special rod as a glob of molten glass.

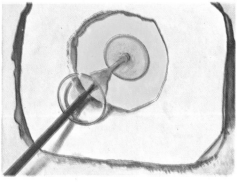

▲ Shaping the finished article is a delicate operation requiring great skill.

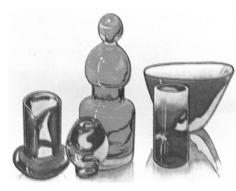

▲ Lustrous and gleaming, these are articles for the luxury market.

▲ Italy has a very important fashion industry. Fabrics, designed in Italy, are elegant and distinctive. Fashions, for both men and women are dramatic and often daring.

Making pasta at home

▲ Pasta, which originated in China, is made of flour, eggs, water and oil.

▲ Mixed and made into an elastic dough it is rolled into very thin sheets.

▲ Then it is cut into strips as here, or shapes, and dried.

Some types of pasta

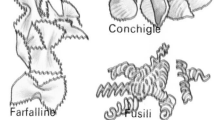

Spaghetti

Ravioli

Canneloni

Conchigle

Farfalline

Fusili

▲ Pasta is not just noodles and spaghetti. It comes in a great variety of shapes and sizes.

From Roman roads to autostrade

Road and rail

The shape and high mountains of Italy have always made transport a major problem. The system of the *autostrade*, or motorways, which provides a network of wide roads through the peaks and valleys is one solution. As in France, one pays a fee to use them. Sixty per cent of Italy's railways were destroyed in World War II, but the Italian State Railways have carried out a plan of rebuilding and now more than half the tracks are electrified. A large number of passengers still use the railways, despite competition from the motor industry. There are connections, often from handsome and very functional stations such as Rome's *Termini*, with all the great European cities.

Sea and air transport

Maritime traffic is heaviest at Genoa (mainly for cargo) and at Naples (mainly for passengers). Along with Trieste, Venice, Palermo, Ancona, Leghorn, Bari and Savona these ports are of immense economical importance. The Italian Merchant fleet now numbers more than 4,000, of which a third are oil tankers. Shipbuilding is an important industry and vessels are built for many countries besides Italy at Genoa, La Spezia, Trieste and Castellamare, south of Naples. A system of canals is planned for completion in 1980.

Alitalia is the state-operated international airline which operates throughout Europe and to many cities further afield.

▲ High speed trains are called *rapido* and ply between the major cities. Service is fast and frequent over 17,000 km. of track.

▼ A bus stop in Rome at the Piazza San Sylvestro. Buses operate on a flat rate and in most cities fares are kept low.

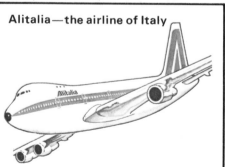

Alitalia—the airline of Italy

The state-operated airline of Italy is Alitalia. The airline has almost 100 jet carriers and its routes cover principal cities in all nations. Alitalia flies out of Leonardo da Vinci Airport (also known as Fiumicino), Rome, the busiest airport in Italy. The domestic airlines ATI and ITAVIA serve the islands, as well as cities on the mainland.

▲ In Rome taxis have special rights of way not allowed to private vehicles.

▲ Italian *autostrade* are miracles of modern engineering. They sweep over the difficult terrain often on high supports as seen here. The new motorway near Bolzano is particularly dramatic and exciting. After Germany, Italy has the best superhighway system in Europe. All roads and traffic circulation are controlled by the State Highway Authority.

► Modern ferries operate between the mainland and the many islands surrounding the Italian peninsula. Here a car ferry is seen approaching the mainland from Sicily. The services between the romantic islands of Ischia, Capri and Elba are heavily used by tourists.

The Fiat story

► The Fiat factory is based in Turin. It started mass production in the early 30s and, in 1938, made the first of the mini-cars, known as the Donald Duck, or Topolino. Now one of the largest car manufacturers in the world, Fiat produces a range of quality cars from the familiar small saloons to fast sports cars and limousines.

The first Fiat—3½ H.P., 1899

Fiat is Italy's most famous and largest builder of automobiles and other machines. In 1903 it began commercial vehicles other than private cars and has gone on to producing aircraft (1915), tractors (1919), railway cars (1931), earth moving machines (1950), electronics (1957), nuclear energy (1958) and space research in 1963. In the company's first producing year, 1900, 24 cars were produced: by 1971 the total of units to come off the assembly lines was 1,589,000. Fiats are an important part of Italy's exports.

A modern Fiat sports car

Rome
the eternal city

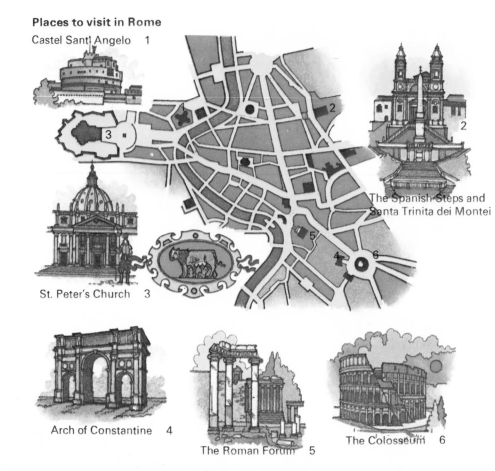

Places to visit in Rome

Castel Sant Angelo 1

The Spanish Steps and Santa Trinita dei Montei 2

St. Peter's Church 3

Arch of Constantine 4

The Roman Forum 5

The Colosseum 6

Famous buildings

Rome is one of the most famous and fabled cities of the world. After the decline of the Roman Empire it lost its importance as a capital, but it has always been the centre of the Roman Catholic faith.

Along with throngs of modern tourists, pilgrims still flock to Saint Peter's. This masterpiece, built by Bramante and Michelangelo, marks the grave of the saint and first bishop of Rome. The piazza of the cathedral, by Bernini, is one of the most impressive sights of the city. It is set between St. Peter's and the Castel Sant Angelo, a medieval fortress that was once the burial mound of the great Emperor Hadrian.

Many Roman buildings can still be seen including the Forum, the Colosseum and the great domed Pantheon. Most of these great monuments of antiquity were stripped in later centuries when popes, cardinals and princes built new churches and palaces. The Colosseum is still enormous, although it has lost half its bulk; it was once overlaid with fine pale marble slabs.

A handsome city

According to tradition Rome began when Romulus and Remus, suckled by a wolf-mother, built the city upon seven hills. An Etruscan statue of the wolf and babies can be seen on the Capitoline Hill where live wolves are still caged as a reminder.

After the conquest of Carthage, Rome dominated all the Mediterranean lands and did not meet bad times until its fall in 476 A.D. Later, in the middle ages, prosperity came again, and the Renaissance brought a great flowering in art and literature.

The city is situated in the wide plain of the River Tiber, not far from the sea. Visitors probably know the Spanish Steps best, but in the dusty heat of a Roman summer its citizens prefer a stroll in one of the many parks, such as the Borghese Gardens.

▲ Along the fashionable arcades of Rome and all principal cities one finds elegant cafés, often with an orchestra.

▶ The Forum is one of the sights of Rome. Seen here dramatically floodlit it stretches to the Colosseum and the Arch of Titus.

▲ Modern Japanese tourists in kimonos before the facade of Saint Peter's.

▶ From the roof of the great cathedral of St. Peter's one glimpses the Tiber and the low skyline of Rome. At left is the drum-shaped Castel St. Angelo.

Roman traditions

▼ In backstreet restaurants you can eat good meals, right on the pavement.

▲ Among Roman ruins in the city live well-fed stray cats.

▶ The famous Trevi fountain fills the side of a small piazza. Coins are thrown in to bring luck.

The magnificent Medici

The rise to power

In 1434 the people of Florence called upon Cosimo de'Medici to rule their city state. Already the Medici had become the leading family in the state through their business interests and moneylending.

Cosimo was humane and an admirer of classical learning and architecture. He eased his conscience over his moneylending (viewed as usury by the church) by building a friary and the church of San Spirito. When Cosimo died, Florence was famous for new ideas and great wealth and since Cosimo's guidance had been decisive, his son and then his grandson ruled.

Lorenzo the Magnificent

The grandson of Cosimo became famous as Lorenzo the Magnificent. He had exactly the same rights as other citizens but his authority was immense. He acted as a statesman, but was also interested in farming, philosophy, writing poetry, and he founded an Academy of Platonists which had important effects on religious beliefs. He also opened his garden to the public to show the artistic works which he and his father had collected. This was the first museum. As a boy, Michelangelo entered Lorenzo's sculpture school and was befriended by him.

When Lorenzo died, much mourned, in 1492, his son Piero followed him and another son became Pope Leo X. Leo continued the building of St. Peter's and commissioned works from Raphael.

Decadence and decline

After a brief period as a republic, Florence was forced to accept a duke, another Medici, Cosimo II. Although the second Duke Cosimo ruled wisely for close on forty years, the old tolerance had gone.

The Medici line became steadily more decadent and perished with the hideous Gian Gastone in 1765. The last grand dukes owed their thrones to spies and Spanish guns. The Medici of the seventeenth and eighteenth centuries had lost the enlightened glory of the first members of that famous family.

▲ Cradled in a curve of the River Arno, Florence has always been an impressive city. Crowded with great buildings, Giotto's bell tower, the cathedral and many palaces, it saw the growth of a new humanism after the dark ages.

◄ Lorenzo de' Medici, first citizen of Florence, was not a handsome man. But his intelligence, generosity and wisdom earned this Medici the title of "Magnificent".

▼ Lorenzo was a great patron of the arts. Paolo Uccello painted the Battle of San Romano in three sections for the Medici palace. With its bright, toy-like colours it illustrates Uccello's discovery—perspective.

▼ Savonarola, a fanatical monk, gained power when the great Lorenzo died. He burned pictures and manuscripts as "vanities" but was himself burned (below) in 1498.

▲ Much of Renaissance Florence still exists, development being confined to the outskirts. However, World War II destroyed all the bridges except the Ponte Vecchio.

▲ Niccolo Machiavelli wrote one of the most important books of the Renaissance—*The Prince*. This early treatise on politics is still read today, even though written for a figure of 400 years ago, Cesare Borgia. "Machiavellian" means to be cunning and unscrupulous.

The birth of a nation

Young Italy

Il Risorgimento means The Resurrection, and the name came originally from a crusading newspaper of the same name. It was edited by Count Camillo Cavour of Piedmont, one of the men who started Italy on its path to unity and independence. The leading patriot was Giuseppe Mazzini, an earnest, idealistic man born in Genoa in 1805, who founded Young Italy, an organization dedicated to the great purpose of making Italy into a nation of free and equal citizens.

In the 1830s, the 18 million Italians were divided into seven states—Lombardy-Venetia, Tuscany, Parma, Modena, all ruled by Austria; the Kingdom of the Two Sicilies in the hands of the Spanish Bourbons; the Papal States headed by the Pope; and Piedmont-Sardinia. Italy was not only divided; it was virtually owned by foreign powers.

When a new pope came to the throne in 1846 a liberalizing effect was felt throughout Italy, although the Pope quickly backed down. Two years later there were successful revolutions against ruling houses in France and Austria and the people of Milan, who had suffered most under Austria, rose up and, along with Venice, threw out the overlords.

Garibaldi—revolutionary fighter

A republic was founded in Rome when the people saw that Pope Pius IX would not follow the national cause. Mazzini took up the government, assisted by Giuseppe Garibaldi, recently arrived from a long exile in South America. But after initial successes, the patriots were scattered by the Austrians.

In Piedmont, however, Cavour became prime minister in 1852. Unlike Mazzini, he was a politician and a monarchist, but neither of them believed that peaceful reforms, with the Pope as head of state, could work. Cavour connived with France, giving up Nice and the Savoy in return for troops.

Again Italy was defeated, and it was Mazzini who saw that if insurrection started in Sicily and worked north, the hated Austrian might be ousted. So it was to be. In 1860, revolution fired afresh in Palermo and soon Garibaldi was on his way.

His first incredible successes attracted thousands to his Redshirts. Then he took Naples, and Victor Emmanuel marched south to be greeted by Garibaldi as "the first king of Italy". Unfortunately both Garibaldi and Mazzini were to live in voluntary exile. Unification was a fact: but Mazzini's dream of an Italian republic was not to come true for many decades.

▲ With his high domed head and enormous intelligence Giuseppe Mazzini was the guiding genius of the Risorgimento. Alas, for his pains he lived in exile after unification.

▲ Camillo Cavour was an unprepossessing man but a brilliant politician. He did not at first foresee unification, but worked to unite the north under Piedmont-Sardinia.

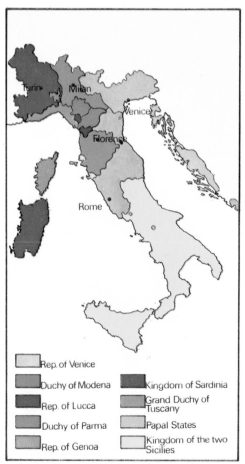

Turin Milan
Venice
Florence
Rome

Rep. of Venice

Duchy of Modena   Kingdom of Sardinia

Rep. of Lucca   Grand Duchy of Tuscany

Duchy of Parma   Papal States

Rep. of Genoa   Kingdom of the two Sicilies

▲ Garibaldi. There is hardly a town in Italy that does not have a square or a street named after this dashing and brave military hero.

▶ The world watched the struggle in Italy, and this cartoon from *Punch* shows Garibaldi helping the king into the Italian boot.

▼ Here Garibaldi can be seen urging on his redshirts at the Battle of Calatafimi. Through this bloodshed the Red Cross was born.

▲ One of the problems of the Risorgimento was the papacy, represented by Pius IX who initially supported uprisings in 1848. However the pope was opposed to unification and would not recognize the Italian state.

▲ San Marino is a tiny city state perched on a mountain top in central Italy. It is an independent country and was not included in the unification of 1870 when the Papal States were annexed.

A turbulent century

Troubled years

In 1870 Rome became the capital of a united Italy. At first the problems were those of organization and recognition, plus the ever-present economic gap between north and south, and the need for social reforms. Then expansion began with the colonization of Eritrea, Somalia, Tripoli and Libya.

Italy joined Britain and France in World War I, making many sacrifices until Vittorio Veneto beat the Austrians in 1918. Although at peace again and with occupied territories restored, Italy faced great social unrest after the war. This frightened the heads of industry, convincing them to finance a new political movement—fascism. Placing its faith in an all-powerful state, the party emerged under Benito Mussolini in 1919.

The rise and fall of Mussolini

At first Mussolini kept the democratic institutions of government, but in 1925 he announced a dictatorship. In 1929 the Pope recognized the Kingdom of Italy and the Vatican State was created. The opposition of the League of Nations to fascism edged Italy closer to an alliance with Hitler. The political climate was becoming threatening. However, realizing that most Italians were against the German alliance, Victor Emmanuel was compelled to arrest Mussolini. He signed an armistice with the Allies, but Germany promptly invaded the north and reinstated Mussolini. Eventually the German armies were routed and Mussolini killed.

In 1946 Italy became a republic and the Royal Family left the country.

▲ The long-delayed treaty between Italy and the Vatican was completed in 1929. Cardinal Gasparri signed on behalf of Pope, Pius XI.

▲ To acquire new territories in Africa Mussolini attacked Abyssinia in 1935. Although the League of Nations attempted economic sanctions against the war, Mussolini continued his offensive and in 1936 he nominated Italy's King as Emperor of Ethiopia. It was a short-lived success for the occupation came to an end in 1941.

▲ Fierce and bitter fighting against Austrian forces took place in the Northern mountains during the 1914-18 war.

◄ In 1922 Mussolini headed the march on Rome having abandoned his former republican convictions for fascism. Squads of armed guards forced the cabinet to proclaim a state of emergency and eventually the king asked Mussolini to form a government. Here the victorious *Duce* is seen with his officers entering Rome's Piazza del Popolo.

◄ Here Signor Mussolini (known as *il Duce*) is seen in Berlin with Hitler. Behind them are Mussolini's son-in-law Count Ciano and General Goering. This picture was taken during the official visit of the Italian Fascists to Germany on September 28, 1937. In 1936 Mussolini began his negotiations with Germany as his hatred of Western liberalism and desire for more territory brought him closer to the Nazis. After secret agreements he met Hitler frequently and in May of 1939 concluded a military alliance with Germany Certain of Germany's success he declared war on Britain and France. This disastrous move lead, in 1945, to his arrest near Como by Italian partisans. As the war was ending in Europe with the defeat of the Nazis, Mussolini was executed.

▲ This ruined village indicates the effects of World War II on Italy. The date is September 1944, and in the rubble-blocked street of Gemmano a British infantryman of the Eighth Army discovers a body—that of one of the many German soldiers who died during the withdrawal.

◄ The end of World War II brought much social upheaval. After the abdication of King Umberto, Italy became a republic in 1946 when this picture was taken. Workers demonstrate their communist sympathies at Arezzo in a demand for work. Italy still has the largest communist party in the West.

A love of romance and humour

▲ Romulus and Remus founded Rome in 753 B.C. Legend says they were suckled by a she-wolf. This Etruscan statue can be seen on the Capitoline Hill, where live wolves are kept.

In Sicily lived the mythical Cyclops, while Vulcan's forge was supposed to be in the very furnace of Mount Etna. Yet these legendary figures grow pale beside the real ones. Dante of Florence suffered exile as a result of his beliefs and died far from his beloved city, yet still he had written the *Divine Comedy* which caused the dialect of Florence to become the national tongue.

St. Francis of Asisi is today beloved everywhere, yet when he lived he was scorned for renouncing the world and seeking to learn from simple creatures. He is always pictured with birds and animals because of his poem, *In Praise of the Creatures* which also used Italian instead of Latin.

Later came such dashing figures as Cellini and the brilliant, ruthless Borgias. Today American style comic characters top the polls, but Italy's own swashbuckling heroes remain to delight people all over the world.

▲ Carlo Collodi created Pinocchio the wooden puppet whose nose grew every time he told a lie. When he promised the Blue Fairy he would not lie again, wishing to be a real boy, woodpeckers cut his nose to size.

▼ Benvenuto Cellini is one of the dynamic men of the Renaissance. Conceited and quick tempered, arrogant and shameless he was yet one of the greatest goldsmiths the world has known. Nothing gave him more pleasure than creating a work of art in precious stones and metals. He fell during a daredevil escape from the Castel St. Angelo in Rome (as illustrated) and then he exchanged his cell for the dazzling court of Francis I, the French king who had offered sanctuary to Leonardo. Back in Florence he created a famous statue of Perseus.

▲ Nobody knows if Juliet existed, but in Verona there is a house with a balcony that is supposed to be hers: Romeo and Juliet are easily imagined in this setting.

▼ Giovanni Cassanova was a swashbuckling figure of the eighteenth century. His amorous adventures have made his name a household word for a great lover. At different times he was a diplomatist, journalist, preacher, musician, gambler and businessman. He travelled widely throughout Europe, frequently leaving a country hurriedly after some scandal or intrigue. In his *Mémoires,* he told of his reckless affairs and violent duels which were a result of his escapades. The book reflects an age when gentlemen had little to do and ladies enjoyed flirting.

▼ The Red Devil, known as *L'incredible devil,* is a very popular comic book hero who started life in America but whose exploits also amaze many young Italians.

▲ This may look like Donald Duck, but in Italy the famous Disney creation is known as Topolino and with other characters from the cartoons is seen everywhere.

The Italian character

The Italian image

No Italian sees himself as an Italian. Even after a century of being an undivided nation, a man from Naples is first a Neapolitan, a citizen of Venice is a Venetian. On a television interview, film director Franco Zeffirelli said "I am not an Italian. I am a Florentine!" However, although Italians are proud of their history, they are also able to see the comic side of things. When all work ceased on a major construction site, to the despair of local people who lost their jobs, they made a joke of it: An old man was left alone on the site with a wheelbarrow. "What have you got there?" chaffed the neighbours, "A gramophone to play construction noises for us?"

The sense of style

Italian men think of themselves as great lady-killers and as possessing immense virility. But it is only fair to say that Italian virility can mean hours spent at the barbers, lots of hair cream and scents, and extravagant clothes. They believe they are very good at business—and are apt to remark with a smile to European colleagues: "What you really need is a good Italian partner!"

Their sense of humour comes to the fore with the military and they do not see themselves as being regimented like soldiers. Many Italians think their bureaucracy is the worst in the world—and it *is* a very complicated system.

Cars are very important to many Italian men and they like to believe they drive them very well—albeit with much theatricality and many near-misses. They believe they are good sportsmen, but after centuries of believing that nature exists for man, many are beginning to see that a policy of conservation and protection is necessary.

▶ Older men like to be well turned out and gallant, even to such young ladies as this one at a pavement café.

▲ A glass of wine and a game of cards—simple pleasures much enjoyed by men, at home or in the local cafe.

Il tenero Giacomo...

▲ The church is everywhere evident in town and country, sober clerics in contrast to the lively Italian younger generation. Priests are highly respected especially in rural areas.

How Italians see themselves

▲ Italian men often believe they are great ladykillers and very virile.

▲ Italian businessmen like to believe they are well organized and full of ideas.

▲ The waiter in Italy has a great and serious pride in his profession, and believes himself every bit as good as his customers.

▲ The Italians create superb clothes and, with reason, both men and women consider themselves very fashion conscious.

▲ Children are dressed up, petted and adored in Italy and the proud *papa* and *mama* tend to feel they are model parents.

The changing face of Italy

OLA IL N.2
ALTERNATIVA
ORGANO DEL "FRONTE DELLA GIOVENTU'

SOTTO LE FORME ESTERIORI
DI UN GOVERNO DEMOCRATICO
UNA DITTATURA INVISIBILE DOMINA
IL POPOLO ITALIANO

▲ A political poster. Italy has many political parties, strongest are the Christian democrats and the communists, followed by socialists and liberals.

▼ The Common Market (E.E.C.) is a federation of nine member countries. The purpose of the E.E.C. is to reduce and eventually abolish tariffs and trade restrictions between members and to establish a European parliament and currency. Italy was a prime mover of the E.E.C.

Italy and her European partners

Problems and solutions

Like all European countries, Italy faces a time of considerable change. Closer economic union with her neighbours and the rest of Europe has resulted in tremendous expansion in industry and commerce. Tourism, which has always been one of Italy's great sources of income, has increased from a mere two million visitors in 1931 to fifteen times that number in 1969. It remains to be seen if numbers will increase or level out due to higher air fares and oil shortages in the coming years.

North and south

The imbalance between north and south is improving a little and there are many programmes designed to improve the quality of life in the south. The Southern Italy Development Fund seeks to undertake large-scale projects such as land reclamation, irrigation, the construction of water and sewage systems, the building of reservoirs and loans to encourage private enterprise. All of this helps to change the face of southern Italy. But there is still an emigration from the south to the north that has caused overcrowding in many cities, bringing with it unsightly slums.

The old cities of Italy with their narrow streets and antique buildings are not easily adapted to increases in the population of human beings and attendant motor vehicles. Some, such as Orvieto, have had their centres closed to traffic.

The danger from pollution

Italy is a country with fearful pollution problems. Without the controls enforced by countries like Holland, the government faces high costs in dealing with the injurious effects of dying rivers, polluted city atmosphere and overcrowded roads. The sea around Italy is also in danger from industrial wastes. Shellfish were contaminated by sewage, causing cholera epidemics in Naples recently, a warning sign of the dreadful danger from the poisons of modern life. There are now plans to control pollution.

Widespread social changes

The family unit is becoming smaller and the close ties of the matriarchal society are less secure. With the somewhat relaxed attitudes of the Roman Catholic church, birth control is more widely practised (although by 'natural' methods) and even divorce a subject almost taboo until recently, is now looked upon with more of a practical eye.

An increasing prosperity

1963

1974

Italy has in recent years undergone a great change in its standard of living. From being a country dependent on old fashioned aids, she has now adopted a full range of modern gadgetry. In 1963 only 29% of the population had a television set. This had grown to 68% in 1969. Although Italians are still not as well off as most other EEC citizens for domestic equipment, one person in four now owns a car—equalling the ratio in Britain.

▼ The promise of higher wages elsewhere has made many poor people leave their homes. They go not only from the south to the rich cities of the north but also to other countries within Europe. Money is usually sent back to relatives.

▲ Although some families live in modern apartments many still crowd together in ancient tenements in the heart of the cities.

▶ Pollution is a major problem in Italy as shown by these detergent clots on the Lambro River, Milan. Controls are now imperative.

53

Reference
Human and physical geography

The climate of Italy

The climate of Italy varies tremendously along the length of the peninsula. We may think of it as a sunny country, and that is partly true. However, the mountainous regions—a vast part of Italy—are often cold and windswept.

Winters are usually short and mild, summers long and warm, and the rainy autumn is warmer than the spring. In Sicily drought is common.

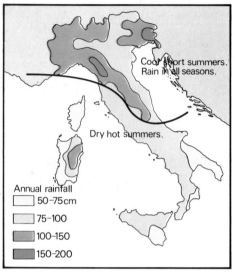

Cool short summers. Rain in all seasons.

Dry hot summers.

Annual rainfall
- 50–75cm
- 75–100
- 100–150
- 150–200

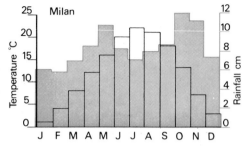

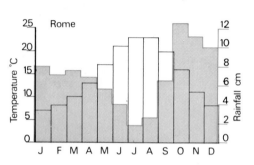

The natural vegetation of Italy

Forest Vegetation
- Mixed Broad-leaved & Coniferous Woodland & Meadow
- Mediterranean Evergreen Forest
- Mediterranean Evergreen Maquis & Meadow
- Mountain Forest

Grass Vegetation
- Grassland

Desert Vegetation
- Alpine

The population density

Inhabitants

per mile²	per km²
under 32	under 12
32-64	12-25
64-128	25-50
128-256	50-100
256-512	100-200
over 512	over 200

The population of Italy

Italy's 56.7 million people are not evenly distributed throughout the peninsula. Many are concentrated within the major cities of Milan, Naples, Rome, Genoa and Turin and their environments. Northern Italy (north of Florence) has almost half the population crowded into a quarter of the area. The north is heavily urban and industrial. The south and central areas with the exception of the big cities, are agricultural. Emigration to the north still goes on, although the more than 100 per cent population increase since Italy's unification (1861) has been evenly spread over all areas. Today Sicily and Sardinia have approx. 13 per cent of the total population.

Population of principal towns (1976)

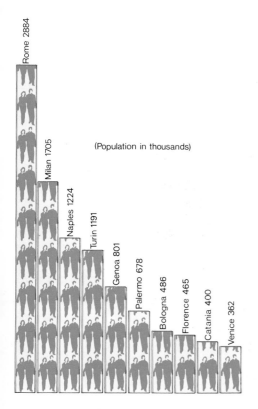

(Population in thousands)

Rome 2884
Milan 1705
Naples 1224
Turin 1191
Genoa 801
Palermo 678
Bologna 486
Florence 465
Catania 400
Venice 362

Government

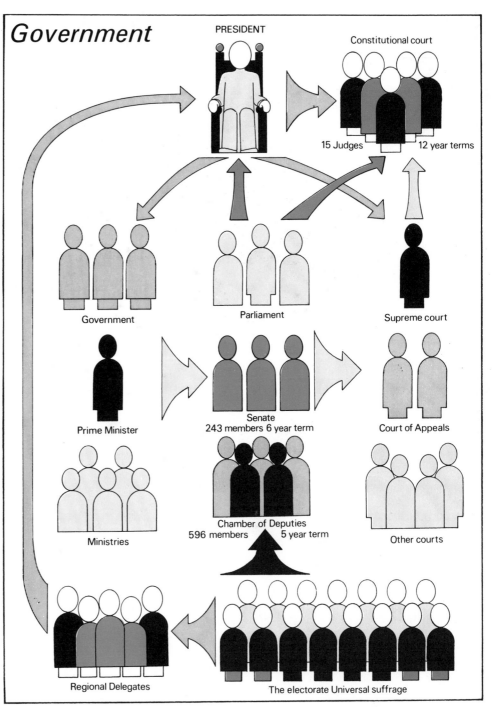

PRESIDENT

Constitutional court
15 Judges   12 year terms

Government

Parliament

Supreme court

Prime Minister

Senate
243 members 6 year term

Court of Appeals

Ministries

Chamber of Deputies
596 members   5 year term

Other courts

Regional Delegates

The electorate Universal suffrage

The Parliament

June 2 is a national holiday in Italy because on that day in 1946 Italy became a parliamentary republic. Government is divided into three branches, the legislative, the executive and the judicial. The president is elected by parliament for seven years. He is Chief of the Armed Forces. He approves bills passed by parliament and may dissolve both Houses to call for new elections. He is not the chief executive, however, for this post belongs to the prime minister, also known as President of the Council of Ministers. These ministers run departments such as the Interior, Foreign Affairs, the Treasury, Education, etc. The Cabinet and Prime Minister can be changed by majority vote of the two chambers at any time.

Local government

In each of the 93 provincial capitals there is a prefect, representing the central government, who is responsible for law and order. He is in charge of the local bodies of the two police forces in Italy—the state police and the Carabinieri. The latter are really a police branch of the army.

Italy has many political parties. Basically an Italian has three choices—the neo-fascists and monarchists on the right, the Christian democrats and allied parties in the centre, and communists and socialists on the left. The strongest party is the Christian democrats. Government since the end of the war has usually been a coalition of this party together with liberals and democratic socialists.

Reference
History

Main events in Italian History

B.C.

10th-5th cents.	Greek colonizing of southern Italy and Sicily.
700	Etruscans arrive in Tuscany.
753	Romulus and Remus found Rome (legendary date).
264	Rome supreme in Italy.
3rd-2nd cents.	Rome extends conquests taking Sicily, Greece and Carthage. Punic Wars.
58-51	Julius Caesar invades Britain and conquers Gaul.
44	Assassination of Julius Caesar.
27	Augustus declares the Roman Empire.

A.D.

98-180	The Golden Century of Peace inaugurated by Trajan.
313	Edict of Milan granting toleration of Christianity.
330'	Constantine moves seat of empire to Constantinople.
376-476	Invasions by Huns, Visigoths, Vandals and Ostrogoths culminating in the destruction of Rome and the end of the western Roman Empire.
529	First monastery in the west founded by St. Benedict at Monte Cassino.
568	Lombard invasions; peninsula divided between Lombards in the north and the Byzantine Empire centred in Ravenna.
755	King Pepin cedes lands in central Italy to the Pope, later to become core of the Papal States.
800	Coronation of Charlemagne as Emperor of the west in St. Peter's, Rome.
mid-9th cent.	Moslem invasions of Sicily and southern Italy.
11th-14th cents.	Rise of the maritime republics (Amalfi, Pisa, Genoa and Venice) and the city states (Florence, Milan, Ferrara and Siena). Guelph and Ghibelline factions emerge supporting either popes or emperors.
11th cent.	Normans invade and oust Moslems from the south. Settle in Sicily and southern Italy.
1309-77	Papacy moved to Avignon during "Babylonian captivity".
1469-94	Peak of Renaissance under Lorenzo de Medici in Florence. Florence is ruled after his death by Savonarola until 1498 when he is burned at the stake.
1494-1559	Age of invasions as Spain and France struggle to control Italy. At the treaty of Cateau-Cambresis Spain gains control of Italy in 1559.
1713	Spanish ascendancy in Italy brought to an end with the War of the Spanish Succession and Austria becomes the dominating power, particularly after the Treaty of Aix-la-Chapelle (1748) confirms her proprietorship of Lombardy and the Veneto.
1796	Napoleon invades Italy, bringing the ideals of the French Revolution.
1797	Venice ends a millenium of independence as she is ceded to Austria.
1806	Austria loses its possessions in Italy but regains them in 1815 after fall of Napoleon and the Congress of Vienna.
1831	Mazzini begins the *Young Italy* movement, insurrections abound. Other patriotic societies flourish in a movement to oust Austria from Italy.
1847	Cavour founds a paper called *Il Risorgimento* in the north, which gives a name to the entire movement.
1848-9	Insurrections in Lombardy and the Veneto put down.
1852	Cavour made prime minister of Piedmont.
1859	War of Liberation. With the help of the French, the Piedmontese defeat the Austrians, gaining Lombardy, Tuscany and Emilia. Northern Italy is thus united, and forms the core of a new Italy.
1860	Garibaldi invades from the south, taking Sicily and Naples. Piedmont annexes the central states of Umbria and the Marches to the Kingdom of Sardinia. Only Venice remains in Austrian hands and Rome held by the Pope.
1861	The Kingdom of Italy proclaimed with Victor Emmanuel II of Piedmont and Sardinia as king. First Italian parliament meets in Turin.
1866	Venice ceded to Italy by Austria.
1870	Unification is completed as Italian troops take Rome.
1882	Triple Alliance formed with Germany and Austria.
1915-18	Italy enters World War I and declares war on Germany and Austria.
1918-22	Economic crises cause rise of the *Fascisti*.
1922	Mussolini marches on Rome, then with the king's consent, forms a cabinet.
1923-4	Mussolini's electoral law is passed. Fascist takeover.
1929	Lateran Treaty creates the Vatican City as a separate state the Vatican recognizes the Kingdom of Italy.
1935-36	Following a policy of colonial expansion, Mussolini conquers Ethiopia, despite League of Nations protests.
1936-9	Mussolini aids Franco in Spanish Civil War.
1940	Italy joins Germany against France and Britain in World War II.
1943	Allies land in Sicily. Mussolini captured. His successor, Badoglio, signs surrender and declares war on Germany.
1945	All of Italy liberated by Allies with the Italian army and partisan movement. Members of the latter capture and execute Mussolini.
1946	Republic declared.
1948	First elections won by Christian Democrats.
1949	Italy joins NATO.
1955	Italy enters the U.N.
1957	Italy joins the Common Market.
1966	Floods inundate Florence, damaging many works of art. Papal encyclical against contraception.
1968	Series of strikes, riots and clashes between right and left.
1970	Divorce bill becomes law.
1971	Riots in Reggio over new capital of Calabria.
1978	Ex-premier Moro kidnapped and killed. Polish cardinal becomes Pope.

The Arts

ARCHITECTURE

Many of the early architects of Italy are unknown. The great monuments of Rome, the early Christian churches (Byzantine, Romanesque and Gothic), are often by the hands of unknown masters and these men often gave rise to whole movements.

Brunelleschi, Filippo (1377-1446): Dome of Sta. Maria dell Fiore, cloisters of Santa Croce, both Florence.

Alberti, Leon Battista (1404-72): Another architect of classic forms— Malatesta Temple at Rimini.

Bramante, Donato (1444-1514): One of the greatest Renaissance architects— responsible for the original design of St. Peter's, Rome.

Sansovino, Jacopo (1486-1570): Venetian architect.

Palladio, Andrea (1518-80): Villas by this genius dot the countryside around Vicenza. His influence is very strong in England.

Bernini, Gian Lorenzo (1598-1680): First great baroque architect was also a sculptor. Works include the colonnade of St. Peter's, Rome.

Borromini, Francesco (1599-1667): Baroque genius who designed churches and buildings that still give Rome its special architectural look.

Nervi, Pier Luigi (1891-): Daring modern architect whose work has influenced many others. Stadium in Rome and Palazzo del Laboro, Turin.

Ponti, Gio (1891-): Designer of the famous Pirelli Building, Milan.

PAINTING AND SCULPTURE

Pisano, Nicola (c.1220-83) and son **Giovanni** (c.1250-1314): Important sculptors of the Gothic period. Church commissions.

Pisano, Andrea (c.1290-1347): Doors of the Baptistry, Florence. Influential sculptor.

Bondone, Giotto di (c.1266-1337): Great muralist, both sublime and human scale in works at Padua, Assisi and Florence.

Donatello (1386-1466): One of the greatest sculptors. His bronze *David* in the Bargello, Florence and *St John the Baptist* are superb.

Robbia, Lucca della (1400-1482): Famed for gentle sculptures of children, angels, madonnas, often in the form of plaques.

Verrocchio, Andrea del (1435-1488): Teacher of Leonardo, produced *Amorini col delfino* fountain, Florence; *Colleoni* equestrian monument, Venice.

Uccello, Paolo (1397-1475): Discoverer of perspective. *Battle of San Romagno*, painting now in three separate parts in three museums.

Francesca, Piero della (c.1420-92): Frescoes and portraits—*Frederico of Montefeltro*. His genius evident in San Francisco, Arezzo, wallpaintings.

Botticelli, Sandro (1444-1510): One of a school of new painters. *Primavera* and *Birth of Venus* his masterworks at the Uffizi, Florence.

Mantegna, Andrea (1431-1506): Paduan painter of renown, strong yet refined figures. *Cristo morto* at the Brera Academy; frescoes at Mantua.

Bellini, Giovanni (c.1430-1516): Venetian painter of great purity and delicacy—*Madonna degli Alberelli*, Brera, Milan.

Vinci, Leonardo da (1452-1519): One of the three greatest artists of the Renaissance. His painting, sculpture and architecture are renowned, but he was also poet, musician, inventor and physicist. *Mona Lisa* (Louvre) the most famous painting.

Sanzio, Raffaello (1483-1520): Raphael's paintings were considered a return to Greek art, their colours glowing, subjects in studied poses.

Buanarroti, Michelangelo (1475-1564): During his long life this great artist worked continuously as painter, sculptor and poet. *Medici Tombs*, Florence; *Sistine Chapel* frescoes and the design for the *largest dome in the world*, St. Peter's.

Cellini, Benvenuto (1500-71): Sculptor in bronze. The *Perseus*, Florence.

Venetian School: Painters such as Giorgione, Tintoretto, Veronese and Correggio although—

Vecellio, Tiziano (1477-1576) is probably the most famous of all. Titian's range as a painter was vast. *Sacred and Profane Love, Self Portrait, Duke of Norfolk,* the *Assunta.*

Caravaggio (c.1573-1609): Strongly lit, often violent paintings showing his great power of expression.

Canale, Antonio (1697-1768): Canaletto's scenes of Venice are famous. He also painted English scenes during visits.

Guardi, Francesco (1712-93): Views of his city of Venice in a more 'impressionistic' style than Canaletto.

Tiepolo, Gian Battista (c.1696-1770): Frescoes and enormous canvases depicting classical legends.

Canova, Antonio (1757-1822): Neoclassical sculptor considered foremost exponent of the style. *Pauline Borghese* as Venus; *Cupid and Psyche*, Louvre, Paris.

Modigliani, Amadeo (1884-1920): Master of modern painting who often painted nudes and portraits of women. Sculptures include *Teste femminili.*

Chirico, Giorgio de (1888-): Painter of metaphysical movement. *Piazza d'Italia.*

Marini, Marino (1901-): Important sculptor often working with mounted figures, horses, in bronze.

LITERATURE

Assisi, St Francis (13th cent.): His one poem, *Cantico delle Creature* is superb; it coincides with the Sicilian School at the court of Frederick II of Swabia.

Alighieri, Dante (1265-1321): Most important of all Italian writers; his *Divina Commedia* is a sublime example of human intellect. This work still inspires research and criticism.

Petrarca, Francesco (1304-74): Petrarch's collection of 366 poems (*Canzoniere*) is perfect in style.

Boccaccio, Giovanni (1313-75): Famous for his collection of 100 tales entitled *The Decameron*, sometimes called the *Human Comedy.*

Humanism: A 15th century movement related to Greek and Latin classical studies. Poets were **Lorenzo de' Medici, Poliziano** and **Jacopo Sannazzaro**. Prose: **Leon Battista Alberti.**

Ariosto, Ludovico (1474-1533): Chivalrous poem *Orlando Furioso.*

Machiavelli, Niccolo (1469-1527): *The Prince* and *Mandragola.* First modern historian.

Bembo, Pietro (1470-1547): Widely imitated in later centuries, Latinist and author of the *Asolani.*

Vasari, Giorgio (1511-74): author of 16th cent. *Lives of Painters, Sculptors and Architects.*

Tasso, Torquato (1544-95): Poem, *Gerusalemme Liberata.*

Goldoni, Carlo (1707-93): Venetian playwright who made written texts of the *commedia dell'arte.* Known as the Italian Molière

Leopardi, Giacomo (1798-1837): Poet of great sensitivity. *I Canti; Operetti morali; Zibaldone.*

D'Annunzio, Gabriele (1861-1938): Poet, dramatist and author. Great influence at beginning of 20th century. Verse—*Le Laudi.*

Pirandello, Luigi (1867-1936): Dramatist who in 1934 won the Nobel Prize. *Enrico IV, Six Characters in Search of an Author.*

Moravia, Alberto (1907-): Novelist (*Gli indifferenti*) and leading literary light.

Lampedusa, Giuseppe Tommasi di (1896-1957): Author of *The Leopard.*

Barzini, Luigi Jr. (1908-): Best seller on Italy and its people, *The Italians.*

MUSIC

Gregorian Chants: The oldest musical documentation in Europe after the 6th cent. (after Pope Gregory).

Arezzo, Guido d' (9th cent.): First example of musical composition on a pentagram and names of seven notes.

Palestrina, Giovanni Pierluigi de (1525-94): First choral mass.

Monteverdi, Claudio (1567-1643): One of the first to combine drama and music in *opera.* Composer of *Orfeo.*

Lulli, Giovan Battista (1632-87): Under the name of Lully introduced opera into France.

Vivaldi, Antonio (c1675-1741): One of the greatest Italian composers. *The Seasons,* many oratorios and *concerti grossi.*

Scarlatti, Alessandro (1685-1757) and his son Domenico. Harpsichord music for the School of Naples.

Pergolesi, Giambattista (1710-36): Opera (*La Serva Padrona*) and choral works. (*Stabat Mater*)

Cimarosa, Domenico (1749-1801): New techniques and *Matrimonio Segreto,* popular opera.

Boccherini, Luigi (1743-1805): Only recently has this composer received full recognition for his quartets and quintets.

Paganini, Niccolo (1782-1840): Master of the violin.

Cherubini, Luigi (1760-1842): Opera and symphonies.

Rossini, Gioacchino (1792-1868): Revitalized flagging opera with his delightful melodies. Works include *Barber of Seville* and *William Tell.*

Bellini, Vincenzo (1801-35): Composer of opera—most famous *Norma.*

Donizetti, Gaetano (1797-1848): Follower of Rossini—works include *Lucia di Lammermoor, Don Pasquale, L'Elisir d'amore.*

Verdi, Giuseppe (1813-1901): Most famous of opera composers. His works (*Aida, Trovatore, Traviata, Otello, Rigoletto* etc.) a staple of operatic repertory everywhere.

Puccini, Giacomo (1858-1924): Another great supplier of top operatic works—*Bohème, Tosca, Madame Butterfly, Turandot, Manon Lescaut.*

Mascagni, Pietro (1863-1945) and **Leoncavallo, Ruggiero** (1858-1919): Mainly known for *Cavalleria Rusticana* (Mascagni) and *Pagliacci* (Leoncavallo) always played as a double bill.

Respighi, Ottorino (1897-1936): Much influenced by earlier composers. Chamber music. Composed *The Fountains of Rome.*

Dallapiccola, Luigi (1904-): Diatonic and dodecaphonic system experimenter. Works include *Partita* and *Volo di Notte.*

Petrassi, Goffredo (1904-): Along with the former the most important contemporary composer. Tonal classicism represented by *Cori di morti.*

Reference
The Economy

Agriculture in Italy

Key:
- Grapes
- Tobacco
- Sugar-beet
- Potatoes
- Rice
- Olives
- Principal Fishing Ports
- Cows
- Sheep
- Pigs

FACTS AND FIGURES

Gross domestic product: (1977) 179,000 billion lire.
Economic growth rate: 2-2½% (estimated rate for 1978).

Main sources of income:
Agriculture: Olives, olive oil, wheat, (second to France in Europe in wheat production), wines, vegetables of all kinds, fruits, nuts, flowers, fodder crops, dairy products, livestock.
Fishing: Anchovies, sardine, mackerel, shellfish.
Mining: Iron, lead, zinc, manganese, bauxite, sulphur, pyrites and mercury
Industry: Tourism, textiles, chemicals, machinery, shipbuilding, iron and steel, motor vehicles, aircraft.
Other products: fashions (clothes, textiles and shoes) marble, furnishings.

Main trading partners: The Common Market countries and the United States.

Currency: The lire. £1 is worth approximately 1,700 lire (1979).

Economic growth

Italy was mainly an agricultural country until 1930. This has entirely changed since World War II when the country swiftly became an industrial society.

Agriculture contributed 32 per cent to the gross national product in 1950: by 1978 it had dropped to 7 per cent. Industrial production increased threefold since the war and tenfold since 1900. This happened although Italy is poor in mineral resources and must import considerable quantities of steel scrap, iron and iron ore.

During the 1970s the economy has grown at an average rate of about 3 per cent per annum. The spectacular growth of the period 1957-67, during which industrial production shot up by 91 per cent, has given way to a tendency for firms to rationalize production rather than investing in new plant and machinery.

Following balance of payments deficits in 1975 and 1976, Italy achieved substantial net surpluses in 1977 and 1978. Surpluses on services, particularly tourism, have made a large contribution, and this was more than enough to overcome the excess of imports over exports in 1977.

Italian imports and exports

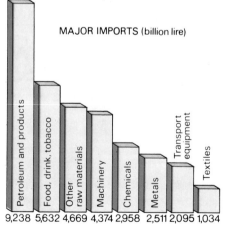

MAJOR IMPORTS (billion lire)

- Petroleum and products: 9,238
- Food, drink, tobacco: 5,632
- Other raw materials: 4,669
- Machinery: 4,374
- Chemicals: 2,958
- Metals: 2,511
- Transport equipment: 2,095
- Textiles: 1,034

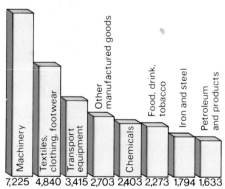

MAJOR EXPORTS (billion lire)

- Machinery: 7,225
- Textiles, clothing, footwear: 4,840
- Transport equipment: 3,415
- Other manufactured goods: 2,703
- Chemicals: 2,403
- Food, drink, tobacco: 2,273
- Iron and steel: 1,794
- Petroleum and products: 1,633

(Figures for 1976) Total imports for the year amounted to over 36,000 billion lire while exports were just under 31,000 billion lire. Imports of petroleum account for nearly twice the difference between imports and exports. Italy must also import many of the raw materials needed for her major exports, which are machinery, clothing and footwear, and transport equipment.

How labour is employed (1976)

Other population

Employed population (19,460,000)

Agriculture

Industry

Others

Military

Total population 56,600,000

15·1% 42·3% 40·9% 1·7%

Although the government publicizes its Green Plan for farmers' credit, workers still drift to the industrial cities. Two and a half times as many people work in industry as on the land and over half the total work force is in services.

Industry in Italy

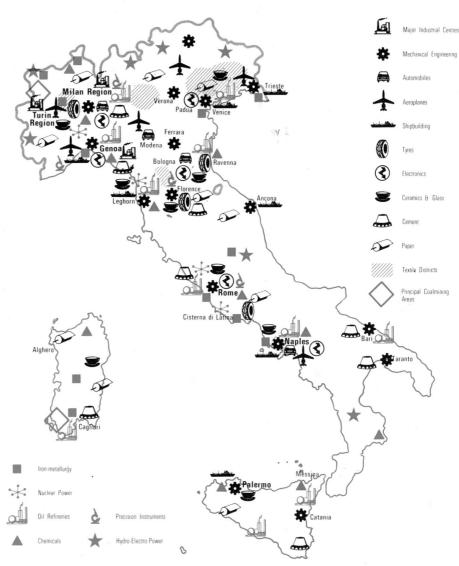

Milan Region
Turin Region
Genoa
Verona
Padua
Venice
Trieste
Ferrara
Modena
Bologna
Ravenna
Florence
Leghorn
Ancona
Rome
Cisterna di Latina
Alghero
Cagliari
Naples
Bari
Taranto
Palermo
Messina
Catania

Major Industrial Centres
Mechanical Engineering
Automobiles
Aeroplanes
Shipbuilding
Tyres
Electronics
Ceramics & Glass
Cement
Paper
Textile Districts
Principal Coalmining Areas

Iron-metallurgy
Nuclear Power
Oil Refineries
Chemicals
Precision Instruments
Hydro-Electro-Power

The goods owned by Italy and the world

(Figures for 1974-75) Italy's standard of living is steadily catching up with other developed nations. But while an increasing proportion of the population have access to modern consumer goods there is still a big gap between rich and poor within the country. In some respects, such as infant mortality rates, Italy is still lagging behind most other western European countries.

(Units per thousand habitants)

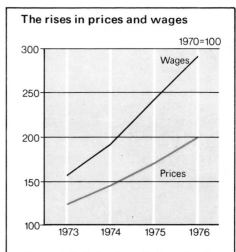

Italy 259
United Britain 379
France 262
Germany 317
Belgium 285
United States 695

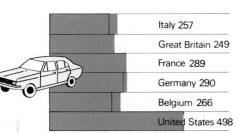

Italy 257
Great Britain 249
France 289
Germany 290
Belgium 266
United States 498

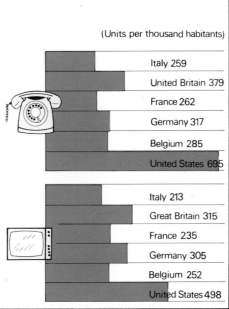

Italy 213
Great Britain 315
France 235
Germany 305
Belgium 252
United States 498

The rises in prices and wages

1970=100

300
250
200
150
100

Wages

Prices

1973 1974 1975 1976

Recently Italy has been in the grip of economic difficulties. However, wages have maintained a general increase although the lira, battered by speculative movements, lost value against other currencies in 1972. Italians now have to pay more for imports and recent inflation has increased food prices.

Gazetteer

Abruzzi. (42 10N 14 0E) Mountainous region. Capital Aquila, 60,000 inhabitants. Sheepbreeding (wool), agriculture, pasturage, fishing (from Adriatic port Pescara, largest town).

Alps. Mountain chain to north and west of the Italian peninsula. Some of the highest mountains in Europe—Monte Rosa (4,638 metres).

Ancona. (43 38N 13 34E) Capital of the Marches. Important sea port built by the Emperor Trajan (110,000).

Apennines. Mountain range running down the entire length of Italy from the north west above Genoa to the southern most point and reappearing in Sicily. Monte Corno highest peak (2,914 metres).

Apulia. (40 40N 17 20E) Region of south eastern Italy. Bari, capital and port (350,000 inhabitants) second largest city in south. Agriculture (centred at Foggia), industry (Brindisi and Taranto).

L'Aquila. (42 20N 13 24E) Capital of the Abruzzi (60,000).

Bari. (41 7N 16 53E) Capital of Apulia. Fishing port (350,000—second largest city in the south).

Basilicata. (40 30N 16 0E) Region; mountainous and poor. Capital, Potenza (53,000). Agriculture, industry at Ferrandina.

Bologna. (44 29N 11 23E) Capital of the Emilia-Romagna (480,000) and home of Europe's oldest university, founded 1135. An Etruscan city, it was vital in the middle ages.

Cagliari. (39 19N 9 8E) Regional capital of Sardinia (211,000).

Calabria. (39 10N 16 20E) Region of high mountains. Capital, Reggio di Calabria (165,000). Citrus orchards, hydro-electricity, tourism.

Campania. (40 50N 14 45E). Region along SW coast, heavily populated with many resorts—Amalfi, Sorrento, Positano. Intensive agriculture, steel, shipbuilding, tourism.

Campobasso. (41 37N 14 44E) Capital of Molise (165,000). Famous for cutlery.

Capri. (40 35N 14 18E) Island, part of Campania region in the Gulf of Naples. Popular with tourists.

Catania. (37 33N 15 7E) Provincial capital in Sicily, coastal town and centre for visiting Etna.

Como. (45 49N 9 8E) One of the northern lakes. Also provincial city.

Dolomites. Mountain range of unusual formations north east. Highest peak Monte Mamolada (3,342 metres).

Elba. (42 50N 10 20E) Island between Corsica and mainland. Napoleon exiled here.

Emilia-Romagna. (44 33N 10 40E) Flourishing agricultural region. Bologna (480,000) capital, important rail junction. Provincial capitals: Modena, Parma, Piacenza, Reggio Emilia, Ravenna, Forli.

Etna. (37 42N 15 0E) Volcano in Sicily.

Friuli-Venezia Giulia. (46 15N 12 50E) Eastern region, two ethnic minorities (Ladin and Slovene) enjoy equal rights with Italians. Capital Trieste (281,000) important port. Agriculture, shipbuilding, oil refining, textiles.

Florence. (43 48N 11 18E) Firenze in Italian, leading art city and cradle of the Renaissance with many museums and important buildings. Capital of Tuscany (436,000). Situated on the River Arno, a centre for craftsmen in jewellery, furnishings, leather goods and fabrics.

Garda. (45 40N 10 40E) One of the northern lakes.

Genoa. (44 25N 8 58E) Capital of the coastal area of Liguria (844,000) an important industrial centre and a port for passengers and goods. Meeting point of the two rivieras.

Ischia. (40 46N 13 54E) Island in the Gulf of Naples.

Latium. (42 0N 12 20E) Region centred about the capital, Rome. Much wasteland (Pontine Marshes, the Campagna) now reclaimed. Viterbo renowned for Etruscan remains.

Liguria. (44 20N 8 30E) Region along Gulf of Genoa. Agricultural crops—olives, fruits, flowers. Shipbuilding and engineering at La Spezia. Tourism.

Lombardy. (45 22N 9 50E) Region marking the greatest concentration of industry in Italy. Intensive agriculture, dairy products, livestock, building. Besides capital of Milan, cities are Cremona, Bergamo, Brescia, Mantua, Pavia.

Maggiore. (46 0N 8 40E) One of the northern lakes.

Marches. (43 20N 13 20E) Region along central Adriatic coast. Capital Ancona, (110,000) important seaport. Important art city of Urbino. Fishing, agriculture and tourism.

Milan. (45 28N 9 12E) Most important banking, commercial and industrial city of Italy. Important road, rail and air junction. Universities, museums and La Scala Opera home. Trade fairs (1,683,000).

Molise. (41 30N 14 30E) Central region, capital Campobasso (40,000) famous for cutlery. Mountainous region.

Naples. (40 53N 14 18E) Napoli in Italian. Capital of Campagnia (1,263,000). Passenger and trade port of great importance. Industrial and cultural centre.

Padua. (45 23N 11 51E) Notable historic and art centre, ancient university, industrial city.

Palermo. (38 8N 13 18E) Capital of Sicily (658,000) with many striking buildings.

Piedmont. (45 0N 7 40E) Region with major industrial works including Fiat. Textiles, agriculture, wines, livestock, food industries.

Po. (45 2N 9 20E) Most important river of Italy, its valley a great agricultural and cultural centre. Po flatlands account for three-fifths of all Italian level land.

Potenza. (40 41N 15 50E) Capital of Basilicata. Centre for olive growing (53,000).

Reggio di Calabria. (38 7N 15 41E) Capital of Calabria, founded 750 B.C. Ferry port for Sicily and the city of Messina (165,000).

Rome. (41 53N 12 33E) Capital of Italy and the largest city in the country (2,700,000). Traditionally founded in 753 B.C. on seven hills, the city was the nerve centre of Roman civilization, for 500 years ruled the entire known world. Seat of government and of the largest university of Italy. Centre for crafts and fashion.

Sardinia. (40 20N 9 5E) Island and region (24,089 sq. kms.). Agriculture, sheep, fishing, tourism. Ancient historical sites (*nuraghi*) and art cities. Coal and mineral mining.

Sicily. (37 40N 14 0E) Region and largest island in the Mediterranean (25,707 sq. kms.). Mild climate, flourishing agriculture, fishing and mineral mining. Oil deposits, petrochemical works. Greek-Roman remains attract many tourists. Palermo (658,000) the capital. Other cities Catania, Messina.

San Marino. (43 58N 12 30E) Independent state situated between Marches and Emilia-Romagna. Oldest state in Europe—founded 301 A.D.

Trentino-Alto-Adige. (46 5N 11 0E) Alpine region and holiday area for the Dolomites. Considerable German spoken.

Trieste. (45 39N 13 50E) Chief city of Venezia-Giulia, important port, mining centre. Annexed to Italy after First World War (281,000)

Tuscany. (43 35N 11 20E) Region, centre of ancient Etruscan civilization. Notable cities Florence (capital), Siena, Pisa, Arezzo, Pistoia, Lucca. Tourism. Mining for minerals. Marble, agriculture. Industrial centre.

Turin (45 2N 7 43E) 1,131,000. Capital of Piedmont and important mechanical and clothing centre. Important road and rai junction.

Umbria. (43 0N 14 40E) Region of central Italy, mountainous) and agricultural. Capital, Perugia (120,000). Steel and chemical plants at Terni, Cultural centres of Orvieto, Gubbio, Assisi and Spoleto. Artisan trades, tourism.

Valle d'Aosta. (45 45N 7 22E) Northern Alpine region, capitol Aosta. Tourism, forestry and hydro-electric plants. French widely spoken. Mining.

Vatican City. (41 53N 12 33E) Independent state within Rome. Residence of the Pope, head of the Roman Catholic Church. Smallest state in the world, approx. 1,000 inhabitants. Created 1929.

Veneto. (46 0N 12 0E) Region of plains to north east. Fine wines, horticultural products, glass, lace, shipbuilding, steel, sugar refining. Notable historic cities of Verona, Vicenza, Padua with its ancient university.

Venice. (45 27N 12 20E) Capital of the Veneto and one of the world's most exquisite cities (347,000). Built on islands along the Grand Canal. Transport by water. Famous and beautiful monuments, museums and churches.

Verona. (45 26N 11 0E) Important city on the Adige. Roman arena largest after Colosseum.

Vesuvius. (40 54N 14 28E) Volcano situated on the Gulf of Naples above Pompeii, the city it buried in its lava.

Index

Numbers in **heavy** type refer to illustrations